Tried by Fire, but Not Burned

Clayton E. Howard

Foreword by Yolonda Tonette Sanders

Yo Productions, LLC
Columbus, Ohio

Copyright © 2015 by Clayton E. Howard

First Edition

All rights reserved. No part of this book may be reproduced or transmitted in any form or by any means without the prior written permission of its publisher. Contact Yo Productions at P.O. Box 32329, Columbus, OH 43232.

Unless otherwise noted, all Scripture references are taken from the Holy Bible, King James Version. Public Domain.

Scripture references noted "NKJV" are taken from the Holy Bible, New King James Version, copyright © 1982 by Thomas Nelson, Inc. Used by permission. All rights reserved.

Some names and identifying details have been changed to protect the privacy of individuals.

ISBN 978-0-9964355-0-5

ISBN 978-0-9964355-1-2 (ebook)

LCCN 2015942791

Yo Productions, LLC
P.O. Box 32329
Columbus, OH 43232
www.yoproductions.net

Cover Design: David Sanders, Jr.

Editor: Rubio Publishing Consultants

For information regarding special discounts for bulk purchases, please contact Yo Productions at 614-452-4920 or info_4u@yoproductions.net.

Printed in the United States of America

This book is dedicated to the memory of my maternal and paternal grandmothers, Bessie Griffin and Gather Woods. You are both long gone to your heavenly home, but your prayers are still being manifested here on earth.

Contents

Foreword ix

Introduction: My Purpose for Sharing 1

Chapter 1: In the Beginning 5

Chapter 2: The Making of "Fast Chili" 9

Chapter 3: The Awakening 15

Chapter 4: The Last Call 21

Chapter 5: The Other Side of Yes 25

Chapter 6: Ministry, Marriage, & Mayhem 29

Chapter 7: Feelings & Frustrations 35

Chapter 8: Covered by Grace 41

Chapter 9: A Second Chance for Love 47

Chapter 10: The Good, the Bad, & the Ugly
of Blended Families 51

Chapter 11: In Sickness & in Health 57

Chapter 12: Another Blended Mess 63

Chapter 13: The End of Our Honeymoon 69

Chapter 14: Growing Pains 77

Chapter 15: Truth, Lies, & Consequences 83

Conclusion: Lessons from the Fires of Life 87

Appendix A: Prayer of Salvation 93

Appendix B: Scriptures Used or Referenced 95

Appendix C: Letter of "Support"............................. 115

Endnotes 117

Acknowledgments

This book would have never been written without God's grace and His love that strengthens me each and every day. Without our Lord Jesus Christ, I would not have made it through any of my trials. The fact that I am able to tell my story is strictly because of Jesus. Without Him, there is no life in the Spirit, healing, changing, or forgiveness.

I am also thankful for the love, support, encouragement, and prayers of many faithful friends and family members.

To my wife, Brenda, thank you for your unwavering support and for cheering me on all the way like no one else could.

To my daughters, Ashley, Kristen, and Brittany, I love you girls so much. I hope that I make you proud as a father.

To my siblings, those resting eternally and those still here to celebrate the release of this book with me, thank you for your unconditional love.

To my mother, the late Rosa Lee Howard, and my father, the late Reverend L.C. Howard, you both instilled so much of the Word in me. Thank you for teaching me about *THE* one and only true and living God who cares about all that concerns us and whose love is unmatched. Without your input and prayers, I would not be here today.

To Mattie Owens who has faithfully served by my side, you have been a godsend. I appreciate you much.

This book would still be an unwritten and unpublished story if it had not been for Yolonda Tonette Sanders's professional input and James Greene who saw the need for the book.

To the members of Ebenezer Baptist Church, there are so many of you who stood by me through it all that I cannot begin to list you by name. Know, from the bottom of my heart, I thank you for your love and support, not only of me, but of my wife as well. I cannot fathom being anywhere else. I want to be at Ebenezer until the Lord calls me home. May He not call me anytime soon!

Loving thanks to God for Dr. Curtis Acer Brown for being my Elijah. You pastored Ebenezer Baptist Church for 41 years and 9 months and paved the way for me. You were a leader of leaders. I am forever grateful to succeed you in your retirement.

Foreword

I've met many pastors throughout my thirty-nine years. Some of them I've liked and some ... well, let's just say that they have confirmed why I am not impressed with people who hold church titles. The bottom line is that I hate arrogance. Whenever I see someone in a leadership position portraying him/herself above others, it gets under my skin. I quickly tune out people who constantly reference their titles or parade around like they should be worshiped. It sickens me that there is so much spiritual hierarchy in the church and not enough humility.

In 1 Corinthians 12 (NKJV), the apostle Paul paints a picture of the spiritual Body of Christ, using the physical body as an analogy. In verses 21-25, he says, **"And the eye cannot say to the hand, 'I have no need of you'; nor again the head to the feet, 'I have no need of you.' No, much rather, those members of the body which seem to be weaker are necessary. And those members of the body which we think to be less honorable, on these we bestow greater honor; and our unpresentable parts have greater modesty, but our presentable parts have no need. But God composed the body, having given greater honor to that part which lacks it, that there should be no schism in the body, but that the members should have the same care for one another."**

Rarely is 1 Corinthians 12 lived out in our modern-day churches. It seems like many leaders have forgotten that the purpose of using our spiritual gifts is so that **"God in all things may be glorified through Jesus Christ..."** (1 Peter 4:11). Being used by God doesn't make anyone a "god." Yet, we often find those in church leadership positions, particularly pastors, with a god-like mentality. These are the types who are full of themselves and will be condescending to anyone who doesn't play the worship-the-pastor game. Unfortunately, I've had more experience with prideful leaders than with humble ones. I guess that's why the humble ones stand out in my mind. Such is the case with Pastor Clayton E. Howard.

I had no idea what to expect in the spring of 2013 when I first met Pastor Howard one Saturday afternoon. My third novel, *In Times of Trouble*, had recently been published, and it was a big deal for me. It had been several years since I'd had a new book release, and I wanted to celebrate with the people in my hometown of Sandusky, Ohio. My dad lived there and attended Ebenezer. He spoke with Pastor Howard who gladly opened the doors of the church so I could do a book signing.

I was aware of the drama that had taken place at the church. Quite frankly, I thought it was ridiculous for people to involve the public in what seemed like a private church disagreement about expansion. I believed that those members who were opposed to Pastor Howard's leadership should have gone to another church instead of causing such a ruckus that spilled over into the media and the courthouse. I don't recall my father speaking to me about what was going on until well after Pastor Howard and I had met and gained a mutual respect and admiration for one another. Thus, my assessment of the church matter that I knew very little about then wasn't in defense of Pastor Howard, per se. It was more about how all the commotion was making the Body of Christ look, in general. So many people are already skeptical of church and question whether or not the concept of salvation is fact or fallacy. I thought the drama was only adding to their confusion. Furthermore, it damaged the witness of all of us who claim Jesus as our Lord and Savior. It's hard to tell people about the love of Jesus and why they need Him in their lives when "church folk" are acting messy.

At that time, I had no idea if the accusations against Pastor Howard were true. Either way, I suspected that he must have been an okay person since my dad continued to be a member of the church throughout the craziness. My dad isn't a fool. Perhaps it was my love and respect for my father that allowed me to keep an open mind when he suggested Ebenezer as a place for my book signing. Left on my own, I would have stayed clear of having my name associated in any capacity with Ebenezer or Pastor Howard simply because I don't like drama, in general. I *especially* don't like church drama! My father seemed so excited to have secured the location that I agreed without voicing any of my reservations. My plan was to meet Pastor Howard, thank him for allowing me to have the signing, and silently pray that, if he was a crook or any of the other things he was accused of being, God would convict and change his heart.

Foreword

Immediately, I was taken aback by Pastor Howard's kindness. Not only was he kind to me, but I observed the way he interacted with others. He didn't strike me as the type of pastor who sat back and ordered everyone else to do things, but one that got down in the trenches with his congregants. The pleasure of meeting Pastor Howard was only exceeded by meeting his lovely wife, Sister Brenda.

A year after that signing, I was back at Ebenezer for other events. It was during the subsequent visits when Pastor Howard began to ask me about writing and publishing. Little did he know that the Lord had been tugging on my heart to start the publishing division of Yo Productions. I don't recall how we got into his story and my vision, but we did, and thus began a new walk of faith for both of us. We worked on this book together for over a year during which time I learned a lot about Pastor Howard. He was extremely transparent. He shared the good, the bad, and the ugly of his life, some of which you will be privy to as you read through these pages. This book is a remarkable journey of an ordinary man who connected with an extraordinary God. Pastor Howard is not a man who lacks humility *or* greatness. I found him to be a man of integrity and abundant faith. He encouraged me throughout the entire publishing process. There were times when my nerves would get the best of me and I would admit my fears to him about publishing and the uncertainty that came with it. With his country-twanged voice, he would say, "You're gonna do just fine, baby. I have all the faith in the world in you." I would laugh and reply, "I hope you have more faith in Jesus!"

Pastor Howard does have faith in Jesus. That was evident throughout our many conversations. It is with great pleasure and absolutely no hesitation that Yo Productions presents to you, *Tried by Fire, but Not Burned* by Pastor Clayton E. Howard of Ebenezer Baptist Church in Sandusky, Ohio.

With Honor,

Yolonda Tonette Sanders

Essence Bestselling Author of *Soul Matters*, *Secrets of a Sinner*, and *Wages of Sin*

Yo Productions, LLC — Founder and CEO

Introduction: My Purpose for Sharing

It was April 17, 2014 when the dream of producing this book became a reality. On that day, I had a meeting with a young lady who had previously agreed to help me with (and later publish) it. Both of us were nervous as we gathered together in a small room to discuss the possibilities. She was starting a new publishing venture and I was at the tail end of one of my most challenging experiences since accepting God's calling on my life to preach. It was a painful ordeal that I will never forget, and one that I wouldn't wish on my worst enemies. Yet, it also served as a catalyst for my beginning this book. In it, I share many events that God has used to get me to the point I am at today.

I'm not vain enough to think that you have nothing better to do than to read about my life. Thus, the purpose of this book isn't to share simply for the sake of doing so. There are things that I would rather you *not* know about me, but they were necessary for me to include in order to remain true to the reasons why I chose to write this book in the first place. It is my hope to encourage you through your current and future trials, and also to reaffirm that, despite your past, you still have value and can be used by God. I'm living proof.

As you will soon see, I don't have a "clean" past. I wish I could tell you that all of my sins were before Christ came into my life. That would be a lie. I start with the days prior to my salvation, but I have also made huge mistakes after accepting Jesus. I'd also be lying to say that concern about what people will think about my pre- and post-Christ decisions didn't cross my mind. Of course, it did! I reveal some things that I thought would be kept only between Jesus and me. Again, in order for the goal of this book to be accomplished, I had to share them publicly.

Don't be mistaken. I didn't put *all* of my business in this book, but I've put enough in it to take me way outside my comfort zone. I find that being in ministry does that to me quite often. Yet, there's never been a time when I've been uncomfortable that it has been in vain. God has used my discomfort to bring glory to His name. I believe this book will be no different. That, alone, gives me peace.

As a result of living in this world, we all end up wounded to some extent, some more than others. Many of us like to say that our wounds were caused directly or indirectly by what someone else did or didn't do to us. This can certainly be true. What's equally true is that some of our wounds have also been self-inflicted through bad decisions that we've made. I reflect on my life and I know, without a shadow of doubt, that God has covered me when I was doing right *and* when I wasn't. I should be dead, but I'm not. I should have HIV, but I don't. I should be in prison, but I am free.

At the end of each chapter, you will find questions that coincide with the material presented. It is my hope that you will answer each one honestly. They are exactly as titled . . . your *personal reflections*. If you are reading this book as part of a study group and want to share with other members, then please do so. However, if you're uncomfortable sharing, then please don't feel obligated to do so. Ultimately, your answers are between you and God. I encourage you to be honest with Him. If this book touches on any area of your life, I pray that you'll be transparent with Him so that He can help you make any needed changes.

I hope you're ready to venture through these pages and learn the ugly truth about how I came to the place where I am today. A place of peace, passion, and purpose. A place that I could only be as a result of divine intervention. Perhaps, as you read, you'll see yourself or loved ones in some of the stories.

There are three main things that I want you to get from this book. The first is that no one is beyond God's reach; not your child . . . your sibling . . . your parents . . . your spouse . . . not even *you*. The second is that regardless of your past or recent mistakes, you still matter to God. He's never nor will He ever stop loving you. Whether you're in your twenties, forties, or sixties plus, it's not too late to begin letting God direct your path. I can tell you from experience that resisting Him only causes frustration. It's much easier to surrender to His will.

Finally, I want you to know that your pain is not without purpose. Like the three Hebrew boys in Daniel 3 who were physically thrown into a fire, you may find yourself in a spiritual blaze and the heat may be much more than you think you can withstand. My friend, no matter how "hot" things are, it is possible, with the help of God, to come out of the furnace without being singed or smelling like smoke.

Personal Reflections

1. What are some wounds you have as a result of your life experiences?

2. Would you classify your wounds as being self-inflicted or caused by others?

3. What steps, if any, have you taken to begin healing?

Chapter 1: In the Beginning

My parents moved to Columbus, Ohio from Williamson, West Virginia when my mother was pregnant with me. They came so she could find work. My father, a pastor and a coal miner, had been off because of the strikes. Dad would eventually return to work and commute back and forth from Ohio to West Virginia until years later when he and Mama divorced around the time I was in the eleventh grade. But, I'm jumping ahead. This chapter is titled "In the Beginning." My start on earth came July 29, 1953 when I entered this world as the sixth, and undoubtedly the worst-behaved, of the seven children Rosa Lee Howard birthed.

Some kids can blame their wayward ways on their childhood. I cannot. I came from a close-knit family. Despite my father's commute and my parents' divorce, I had a great relationship with both of them and my siblings. Again, I was the sixth. Mama had been married previously. From her first union, she had my brother Charles (deceased) and my two sisters Bessie and Sue (deceased). After Mama married my dad, Lawrence whom she called "Noley," they had Gloria, Dreama, my younger brother Lorenzo (deceased), and me.

To say that I was the worst-behaved of us all is no exaggeration. Sure, my siblings had their fair share of issues, but none of them gave our mother grief to the extent that I did. I was rebellious to the core. Sometimes it seemed like I did things just to do them, without rhyme or reason. For instance, as I child, I knew that playing with fire could be dangerous. Yet, I did it anyhow. One day I was with a friend, whom I will call Timmy, in the attic playing with matches. We would light them up, let them burn out, and put them aside. When we had finished entertaining ourselves, we left and went to play in my bedroom. Lo and behold, we heard a crackling noise. Long story short, the attic had caught on fire.

Luckily my mom was getting off the bus around the same time and was made aware of the situation. The fire station was down the block from our home, so it didn't take the firemen long to get there either. Timmy and I sat frightened in my bedroom because we knew we'd been the ones to cause the fire. My mom coaxed us out of the house and the firemen quenched the flames. The entire attic was burned as well as a good portion of the house. I didn't know it then, but perhaps that was a prelude to this book's title. I was in a fire back then and managed to escape unharmed.

There were many times as a child that I'd decided to run away from home. I had no good reason to do so. I wasn't being neglected or mistreated in any way. If I got angry, didn't get my way, or simply felt like doing so, I attempted to run away. Most of the time, I came to my senses before getting too far. However, on one particular occasion when I was twelve, I, along with a friend, decided to steal my sister Dreama's 1962 Chevrolet Covair and go to West Virginia to my father's house. My parents were still married at the time. My dad held residence in two states because of work and churches he pastored.

I only stand about five feet, six and half inches now as a man in my early sixties. Clearly, I'm not what one would consider tall. I was even shorter at age twelve and I had very little driving experience. Miraculously, I managed to make it all the way to West Virginia. I think it was quite an accomplishment considering my height, age, lack of a driver's license, and the fact that this was *way* before the invention of the GPS. If I would have possessed even an ounce of common sense, I would have known better than to leave one parent's house and go to the other parent's home in a car that I stole from my sister. My dad did not welcome me with open arms. He disciplined me severely. Use your imagination, if you will, about what that means. There's an adage that says, "A hard head makes a soft behind." My head was sho'nuff hard growing up; that day, my behind was good and soft!

These are some of the crazy things I did in my rebellion. There were plenty of others. Looking back on my childhood, I see that there was a battle between good and evil inside of me. On one hand, I resisted any and everything godly that my parents tried to instill in me. On the other, my favorite thing to do was to play church. I have memories of being as young as five or six years old in the living room of our three-bedroom home on the corner of Long Street and Ohio Avenue (the same one that Timmy and I caught on fire) preaching my "sermons" for hours on end. Sometimes I'd be by myself listening to gospel recordings. Other times, I'd get Gloria and Dreama to go along with me and sing in the "choir." They'd give an A and B selection and then I would come with the "message."

I had no clue back then that I wanted to be a preacher. In fact, I'd dare say that I didn't want to be one. The fact that I resisted the calling later in life suggests so as well. As a child, I merely imitated the actions of my dad and my great-uncle, Paul, who also preached. Like them, I would get a rag (they had handkerchiefs) and use it to wipe the sweat off of my forehead. Of course, I had to do this when Mama and Daddy weren't around or paying attention. They didn't find anything amusing about my sisters or me playing church. When they caught us, we were scolded and ordered to stop. Nevertheless, I continued to do this until I was about twelve years old. Sometimes I'd take my sermons outside and preach the eulogies of grasshoppers and birds. No matter what I was preaching, my messages always included Jesus being crucified and resurrected. I would hoop, holler, and fluctuate my voice at certain points like Baptist preachers are known to do.

It's ironic that I was such a rebel considering I was drawn to all things church in my playtime. There was a dichotomy of good and evil within me as a young child that I would find myself struggling with even into adulthood. I enjoyed sinning initially. It was fun. Yet, the writer of Hebrews tells us that the pleasure of sin is only for a season (Hebrews 11:25). When my season of pleasure wore off, I found myself wanting to do right and yet still doing wrong. It's like what Paul says in Romans 7:15, **"[F]or what I would, that do I not; but what I hate, that do I."** It was an all-out war between my flesh and my spirit.

We often think that this battle is for the "big" sins like drug addiction or sexual immorality. In actuality, this type of fight can be for things like lying or pride. It can be for anything that has a stronghold on us. For me, it was drugs, promiscuity, and alcohol. I indulged in all of them to the fullest. When the pleasure wore off, I became entrapped.

Personal Reflections

1. What was one of your favorite things to do as a child? Does it relate in any way to what you now do as an adult?

2. How did you break the bondage of any past strongholds in your life?

3. Can you identify any current strongholds in your life?

Chapter 2: The Making of "Fast Chili"

I have been asked if there is any childhood event I can pinpoint that turned me away from God and the church as I got older. I truly cannot think of a single thing. There was no death or traumatic event that I can blame for my attitude in my later years. I wasn't mad at God about anything. I hadn't been sexually abused by anyone in the church nor had there been a death of a loved one so devastating to me that I blamed God. Despite my parents' living situation and ultimate divorce, they were both very active in my life and on the same page when it came to raising us children. Mama didn't talk bad about Daddy and vice versa. There were also no negative influences in our home despite the age differences between my older siblings (the ones Mama had with her first husband) and me. My oldest sister, Bessie, is seventeen years my senior. She helped raise me, along with my brother Charles. Bessie, like our mother, was and is a God-fearing woman who tried to teach me right from wrong. She and I are very close to this day. The only dysfunction I can remotely think of is Charlie's alcoholism from which he later died. Still, I didn't become aware of his issues until I was already set in my ways. In essence, my disdain for all things godly wasn't a result of anything or anyone except me.

It was around junior high when I began losing interest in anything that God and the church had to offer. I saw older kids in high school selling drugs, getting high, and driving around in their fancy cars. This was during the time when Columbus was known for the popularity of Mount Vernon Avenue. Mount Vernon is an historic neighborhood near Columbus's east side. It was a community where African American businesses and social clubs thrived.[1]

All sorts of things took place on Mount Vernon. On any given day or night, there wasn't a shortage of legal or illegal activity happening. It was what we considered "the spot." As a young boy, I paid close attention to the high school kids who looked like they were having fun; much more so than the church deacons who claimed to have the "joy of the Lord" working on the inside of them. It's through my envying the older students that the "world" became attractive to me and I accepted its invitation to partake of its pleasures.

I was only in junior high and was already living the "life." I had drugs, money, and women, who, by the way, were in their mid to late twenties or older. Nowadays, the female would be arrested and labeled as a sex offender and I would be viewed as psychologically damaged. However, I don't view myself as a victim. I wasn't manipulated or abused in any manner. It was what I wanted and I was in full control. (Please note: my statement is in no way meant to condone or encourage relationships between adult women and teenage boys. No matter how one may feel, such is wrong! Period.) I liked the attention I received and the respect I was starting to gain. Once I got a taste of this fast-paced world, church was history to me for sure.

I connected with some much older guys, whom I'll call Freddie and Nelo, who introduced me to drugs like marijuana, purple haze, orange sunshine (acid), and heroin. I jumped so quickly at the opportunity to be wayward because I already had a desire to turn away from my biblical foundation. Remember, rebelliousness had been working inside of me for years prior. If this wasn't so, I would not have been so easily drawn to worldliness. James 1:14 confirms this, **"But every man is tempted, when he is drawn away of his own lust, and enticed."** My new friends didn't have to twist my arm in order to get me to do anything. Like a Poker player making a big move, I was all in.

I met Freddie and Nelo one night at a club. I'd learned how to forge IDs and I would often sneak into bars by myself to hang out and drink. Freddie and Nelo were both drug dealers. They took me under their wings and showed me the ropes. We were in a club parking lot in the car when I first tried smoking what was referred to as a lid of reefer back in the day. A lid was a three finger bag of weed that sold for about fifteen dollars at that time. The three of us would all chip in and split it. I didn't have much money because I was so young, but I would scrape together my portion whenever we got lids. Not two weeks after first trying weed, I realized that I couldn't afford to keep up with smoking. This led to my learning the ins and outs of selling drugs.

The Making of "Fast Chili"

I have no idea what the measurements are for weed now, but, back then, a nickel (five dollar) bag was a capful of Boone's Farm wine. As mentioned moments earlier, a lid cost three times as much as the nickel bag, yet, it contained nine capfuls of weed. I may not have been book smart, but I quickly became street smart. I figured out that I could buy a lid, sell nine capfuls for five dollars each, and make a thirty dollar profit each time. Or, realistically, I sold some and smoked some. Still, I no longer had to come out of pocket to get high. My business venture began supporting my habit.

Once I got good at selling lids, I upped the ante and started buying weed by the pound. I eventually got into selling heroin and a drug we used to refer to as "Bam." Bam was a stimulant that helped suppress appetites.[2] I dated and sold Bam to heavyset women who took it to lose weight. Cocaine was another drug that I sold. McDonald's used to have long coffee spoons that we drug dealers would take in large quantities and use to measure cocaine and heroin. Once it became public knowledge how the spoons were being used, the restaurant did away with them.[3] That was a sad day in the drug world!

The older I got, the more exposure I gained, and the better I became at my craft. Around the time when my parents divorced, I dropped out of high school and selling drugs became my full-time gig. I was so good at it that I became the supplier for Freddie and Nelo, the ones who'd first introduced me to this lifestyle. I got the nickname "Fast Chili" because I was always on the go, running around town everywhere selling drugs. Plus, in the winter, I didn't wear a coat. I was known all over Columbus and even in West Virginia. I wasn't in a "miserable world of sin" as the saints like to say. I enjoyed the pleasures of sin up until the time I knew God was calling me to preach.

Proverbs 20:11 says, **"Even a child is known by his doings, whether his work be pure, and whether it be right."** I was known at home and in the streets to be "bad," though the word didn't carry the same connotation in both settings. In the streets, I didn't back down from anyone. As little as I am, I would pick fights in school. I didn't so much pick them in the streets, but people knew that, if anyone stepped to "Fast Chili", I would step back.

At home, I was simply bad in the negative sense of the word. No one ever drilled that word into me. It was something I instinctively knew because of the way I constantly went against the grain. There was no stopping me. If my parents (or Bessie or Charles) said not to do something, they might as well have saved their breath. If it was something I wanted to do, I did it regardless of what they said or the consequences that followed.

When kids go wild, there's a tendency to blame the parents for lack of discipline. While that is the case in some homes, it wasn't in mine. My parents did their best to keep me from going down the road I traveled. They were married for the majority of my childhood, though they maintained separate households. Daddy worked and lived in West Virginia; Mama worked as a housekeeper and lived in Ohio. Maybe if they were under one roof, Mama would not have had to work so hard and I could have had more supervision. Perhaps, but I'm not sure it would have changed much because what was going on wasn't external, it was within me . . . my own lusts. I know for a fact that there are two-parent households in which both the mother and father are God-fearing and loving people. Yet, the child still acts a fool. Trust when I say that there wasn't a lack of discipline in my parents' homes. Neither Mama nor Daddy spared the rod.

With everything in me, I believe my parents did all that was in their power to keep me from going down the wrong path. I was even sent to live with my father for a while in hopes that my behavior would change. It didn't. I found trouble in West Virginia just as I had in Ohio. I would hear Mama praying for me so hard sometimes that she would scare me. She'd say, "Lord, if you don't change Clay, I'm gonna kill him and send him to You early." All I can say is thank God that the **"effectual fervent prayers"** of the righteous **"availeth much!"** (James 5:16). The Lord eventually did change me and Mama didn't have to spend any time behind bars for taking my life.

Personal Reflections

1. Have you ever been mad at God? If so, why? Did the situation cause you to turn away from Him?

2. Sexual immorality comes in many forms such as fornication,

homosexuality, and adultery. Why do you think so many people still engage in these acts despite the consequences of having sex outside of God's will, which is in a marital relationship between a man and a woman?

3. Did you grow up in a single or two-parent household? Do you feel that this had any bearing on the choices you made as a child or an adult?

Chapter 3: The Awakening

From the time I was in junior high school until I was around twenty, I had it going on, as the kids would say. For the most part, I lived in Columbus. I also spent time in Washington, D.C. and West Virginia. It didn't matter which city/state I permanently called home, truth is, I traveled back and forth frequently between all three for drug runs, women, and everything in between. My rebellious behavior continued until 1980 when I finally accepted the Lord's calling on my life to preach. I was in my late twenties at the time. I'd initially heard His call around 1973 when I was twenty. I ignored it then and I continued to do so on many other occasions.

Different people will give various accounts of how they knew God had called them to preach. Some claim to hear voices or see visions. I can't quite put into words how I knew preaching was what I was supposed to be doing. I was selling drugs and doing all kinds of worldly things, which I knew were contrary to how I'd been taught. It was as if my conscience was catching up to me, making me aware that I was headed in the wrong direction and not fulfilling the will that God had for my life. The heavens didn't open up, nor did I hear a voice calling out to me from the sky. It was more of an inner haunting telling me that I had a greater destiny to fulfill.

As a young adult, I became aware that I was supposed to be preaching. This wasn't when God called me. In reality, the calling preceded the time I was in my mother's womb. In Jeremiah 1:5, God tells him, **"Before I formed thee in the belly I knew thee; and before thou camest forth out of the womb I sanctified thee, and I ordained thee a prophet unto the nations."** Whenever we realize something God wants us to do, it's not like He all of a sudden came up with the idea. It's that we are finally getting up to speed with what He's already purposed for our lives. The wise thing would be for us to quickly accept His calling and trust Him with the details to make it happen. Our lives would be much simpler then. But, like me, many choose to ignore Him. I did, time and time again.

I was enjoying my life too much to give it all up for church permanently. I was living in D.C. at the time with a young lady, Nina, who was my main girl. She was aware that I had others on the side. I was there because I wanted to be away from my parents who were getting on my nerves with all their righteous and moral talk. Even in D.C., I did the good person thing every now and then. A friend invited me to church. I went occasionally to keep folks (i.e., my parents) quiet. If they started in on me about the life I was living, at least I could say that I'd gone to church. In my heart, I knew that wasn't enough.

I'm sure you've heard the saying that going to church doesn't make one a Christian like sitting in the garage won't turn a person into a car. Yeah, I know . . . it's been severely overused and yet, I just threw the analogy out once more, beating a dead horse. Forgive me! I went to church enough that I took pride in not being a C.M.E. member. I went more than on Christmas, Mother's Day, and Easter. Still, I was lost because I had not accepted Jesus as my Lord and Savior. I wasn't willing to be obedient to His call. I wrestled internally because I knew I was living wrong and I didn't want to stop. God's will was that I submit to His design for my life and preach. My will was to party. After hearing the Lord and ultimately ignoring Him, the pleasures of sin began to wear off. I ran from this calling for about seven or eight years, which were some of the worst years of my life to date.

My life began to change drastically after I said "no" to God. Everything began going downhill. I'd been selling drugs since I was in junior high school and, not once did I have any serious run-ins with the law. After turning my back on God, I started getting arrested left and right. It seemed like I was a magnet for the police. I didn't like it. I can't say whether or not I made the mental connection, at that time, that my rebelliousness sparked this. If I did, I still didn't change my ways. There was only one incident I can recall that actually gave me pause.

It was around the summer of 1978. I was in the car with Nina's cousin and a new friend. We were traveling from Williamson, West Virginia to Logan, West Virginia to attend a party. (The two cities are about thirty miles apart.) We'd already been drinking and getting high, so, in essence, we were going to do in Logan what we'd already been doing in Williamson.

About halfway through the trip, we realized that we'd forgotten someone. Nina! I was so intoxicated from drugs and alcohol that I'd forgotten my own girlfriend. I convinced the fellas to turn around so we could go get her.

We were driving reckless, going at least ninety to a hundred miles per hour in a 1972 Pinto. It belonged to my new friend. I refer to him as such because I'd literally only met him earlier that day. I'm quite sure that it was insane to get in the car with someone I barely knew to go hang out at a party in a different city. Rationality had escaped me. More booze and alcohol were calling my name. If Logan was where the party was at, then Logan was where I'd planned to be.

As we headed back in the direction of Williamson, the car hit a guard rail and went airborne. My new friend was thrown through the windshield and was dead on impact. I know this because I heard death take his life. I heard the growling and groaning of a demonic spirit that came for him. It was the most agonizing sound I have ever heard to date. It was like something one would hear in a horror movie, but it was real. I know what I heard. I didn't imagine it. I also felt something satanic possess me that day. Perhaps it was a death wish trying to hinder my calling and kill me prematurely. I don't know. I do know that I lived through the accident without even a scratch. So did Nina's cousin. That was nothing but God.

Reflecting on that day, something else comes to mind. Proverbs 18:21 reads, **"Death and life are in the power of the tongue: and they that love it shall eat the fruit thereof."** Prior to heading to Logan, my new friend had visited his family members to say "goodbye." He was telling people that would be the last time they would see him. Whether he had a premonition of his death or he was speaking flippantly, I'm not sure. What is apparent is that he spoke the words and they came to pass.

We must be careful about the things we speak over and into our lives. Some things come upon us because we invite them into our lives through our words. Now, of course, God has the final say over any and everything that happens. He could have spared the young man's life. In His sovereignty, He chose not to do so. No one will ever fully understand the ways of God. His ways are not our ways, nor His thoughts our thoughts (Isaiah 55:8-9).

When God puzzles us, we must always rely on the words in Proverbs 3:5, **"Trust in the Lord with all thine heart; and lean not unto thine own understanding."** I don't understand why my new friend went around telling his loved ones that they would never see him again. I don't know why he invited me to come to a party in Logan, West Virginia or why I agreed to do so. I don't understand why the Lord took his life and spared mine, along with Nina's cousin. There's a lot of things about that day that I don't, nor will I ever understand. This I know: I heard the sound of death and that day changed me.

I attended my friend's funeral despite the strange feeling that was over me. Witnessing his death left me shaken and I was unable to loose myself of the spirit that had grabbed hold of me. I began to isolate myself from everyone, including Nina. I stayed with my aunt. The only time I would come out of the room was to walk the dog. It seemed like everyone around me knew that something was going on, but they didn't know how to deal with me. I didn't know how to deal with myself. I hadn't told anyone what I had witnessed. I couldn't. I'm not even sure that I'm properly articulating things now; I know I wouldn't have been able to do so back then.

Thankfully, I knew enough to pray and that's what I did. I prayed for over a week. I know the saints like to be all deep and quote John 9:31 about God not hearing a sinner's prayer. I'd dare say to you that it is true, God will not hear the prayers of those whose hearts are wicked against Him. However, David reminds us that God will not despise a broken and contrite heart (Psalm 51:17). My praying to God in my sinful state wasn't with a wicked heart. I was broken and I called on the only One I knew could change things.

I was at my aunt's house in my room, praying for deliverance. I was being tormented by the spirit that had possessed my body. God heard my cry. Something came out of me that shook the entire house. It was as if there had been an earthquake. My aunt had elephant whatnots that fell off her shelf and broke. The screen door also shattered. My aunt came to see what was going on. No one knew what had happened except for Jesus and me. At that time, something left me totally. I like to think of that day as the beginning of my accepting the call. In reality, it would be a couple more years before I would do so fully. That day I had a spiritual awakening. I knew I wanted to change, but I truly didn't know how.

Personal Reflections

1. Reflect on Jeremiah 1:5. Do you know what it is that God has called you to do? Are you currently operating in His will? If you don't know what your purpose is, begin praying for God to reveal it to you. If you do know and are not doing it, ask Him to help you begin to desire those things that He wants for your life.

2. Have you been hesitant to pray about something because you feel like God won't hear your prayers because you haven't been doing all things right? Read Psalm 51:17. Does this help to change your perspective about prayer?

3. I know that I was permanently delivered of whatever had possessed me. Since that time, God has delivered me from other things such as drug addiction and alcoholism. Is there anything from which you can say that you know without a shadow of a doubt that you have been delivered?

Chapter 4: The Last Call

One would think that after being delivered from a demonic spirit that I would have done a complete one-eighty. I knew God had done something within me, but I didn't know what to do from that point forward. I truly wanted to change. I think I was ready for it, but I felt helpless. I sought the assistance of those around me, but it didn't seem like anyone could really help me get my life on track. The church folk were giving me Band-Aid answers like "trust God and everything will be all right." That was good to know, but when a person is lost, as I was at that time, it takes a little more than Christianese to help them find the way. Metaphorically speaking, I needed someone to hold my hand and walk me through transitioning. Perhaps the assumption was that because I had grown up in the church, I automatically knew the steps I needed to take to grow with God. Or, maybe I was simply too spiritually dependent on others to help me get to a place that only God Himself could do. Whatever the case, I, again, started going downhill.

When I didn't get the help I was seeking from the church, I turned to my friends. They were glad to welcome me back into their social circles. I indulged more in worldly pleasures than I had done previously. Things were different, though. I was no longer the happy drunk. Getting high had lost its thrill. The excitement of being with different women had faded. I became bitter and I had a horrible attitude that matched how I was feeling. I didn't care about anything or anyone, including myself. I continued this pattern of behavior for at least a year or more until I got caught for breaking and entering. I was too high to remember everything about my last arrest. The few details I do recall, I will share.

I was with William Dent, a drugging/drinking buddy of mine, and another guy. Nina stayed in an apartment off of Sullivant Avenue on the west side of Columbus. A few doors down from her lived a couple of guys who were known to keep a lot of electronics in their place. William got the idea to break in. I'd been known for a lot of things, but stealing wasn't one of them. Yet, I went along with the idea anyway, despite it being way out of my character. We cleaned them out. Somehow, during the process, I cut my hand on a broken window in the guys' apartment.

I'm assuming our intention was to eventually sell the stolen items. Like I said, I don't remember all the details. In any event, we didn't attempt to get rid of anything that night. After completing the deed, I dropped William and the other guy off somewhere and foolishly went back to Nina's with the stuff still stashed in my car. By the time I returned, the police had arrived and were questioning people. Someone recognized my car as being the one involved in the robbery and I had no good explanation for my bleeding hand. In the end, the police found the electronics in my vehicle. I was questioned, and jailed. I took the fall, refusing to implement either of my two accomplices.

I now believe that going to jail was the best thing for me. It caused me to sober up. One of the things I thought about is how I had nothing to show for my life except my green 1971 Cadillac, which had been impounded. I had side businesses that I'd started. I've always been good with cars and so I had a shop on the corner of Long Street and Ohio Avenue, and another on Main Street and Champion Avenue. Yes, both businesses were funded with drug money. That's who I was back then. Everything I had was bought with the profits of my street job.

Locked up, the businesses were no longer important to me. I didn't know what was. I was trying to find myself. I felt lost. Empty. Columbus wasn't doing it. I needed to get away permanently. I called my mother and pleaded with her to get me out of jail. We'd been through this song and dance many times before, but I promised her that, if she got me out one last time, she would never have to do it again. I can't explain why, but I felt in my spirit that things would be different though I had no real game plan for my life. My mother bailed me out. Eventually, I received probation for my crime. After working things out to have my probation transferred to Washington, D.C., I moved there.

I did what I could to find a new direction in D.C. I was doing better. I had a legitimate job at an auto shop working for an African guy. I was so good at working on cars that the owner eventually gave me an entire floor to myself. Still, old habits die hard and I got back into selling drugs, continuing my reckless behavior though not to the same extent.

Nina joined me in D.C. on occasion. She had children to care for in Columbus and so she traveled back and forth a lot. One Friday night, while Nina was away, I was on the corner of 14th and U streets. I don't know how the area is now, but back then it was known for various illegal activities. I was there to make a new cocaine connection when I was approached by a lady of the evening. (A more blunt way to describe her would be prostitute.) She and I had come to an agreement. In exchange for her services, I would provide her cocaine. As we walked down the street to find somewhere to execute the plan, we saw some evangelists preaching. They had bull horns. As their words were projected, the Lord began to raise them up in a vision. They were elevated, like angels, and they seemed to be talking directly to me. Two things they said stood out very clearly to me. "Behold, I stand at the door and knock," and "This is your last call."

As the words of the preachers rang loudly in my ears, I saw something else in a vision. A brand new 1979 Lincoln Continental stretch limo pulled up. It was black. Inside were stacks of money and gorgeous women who stood holding silver platters of cocaine already lined and ready to be snorted. The devil was with them. I didn't see a red image with horns and a pitch fork as is often depicted in Hollywood. I saw a man. He didn't have a sign that read "devil." I just knew it was him. He presented me with all the things he had to offer — money, drugs, and women in greater abundance than what I currently had. As the devil stood trying to entice me, I heard the voice of God repeat, "This is your last call."

I know . . . some of you are wondering if I was high. Yes, I was. I'd been drinking and smoking the entire day up until the time I saw the prostitute. High or not, I know what I saw and it disturbed me greatly. I abandoned the lady and went back to my apartment and tried to snort as much cocaine as I could. I wanted to erase what I had seen from my memory. Finally, after toiling all through the night, I got up Saturday morning and caught the Greyhound to Columbus. I had a car in Columbus that I wanted to bring back to D.C., but that wasn't why I'd left. I needed to think.

All the way to Ohio, I thought about the vision and the words of the preachers. I got to Columbus late Saturday night. Sunday morning I went to church, wrestling with what I knew was a warning from God. The next day I headed back to D.C. in my car. I was approximately one hundred and twenty miles away from D.C in a place called Breezewood, Pennsylvania. I can only be that exact because I remember seeing a sign. What had taken place that Friday night never left me. The weight of my sins were heavy and I was finally ready to surrender. As I got off of the turnpike, I said, "Lord, whatever you'll have me to do, I'll do it. I can't run anymore." Instantly, it was like a ton of bricks had fallen off of my shoulders. I was finally free from the enemy's grip.

Personal Reflections

1. What is your definition of Christianese?

2. Read Ephesians 6:11-13. Do you belief in spiritual warfare? Why or why not?

3. If you've said "yes" to God about something that He's called you to do, describe how you felt after surrendering. If you haven't yet surrendered to God, do a self-evaluation and ask yourself what it is that's stopping you.

Chapter 5: The Other Side of Yes

In Ezekiel 36: 26-27, God tells the prophet to speak the following words to Israel, **"A new heart also will I give you, and a new spirit will I put within you: and I will take away the stony heart out of your flesh, and I will give you an heart of flesh. And I will put my spirit within you, and cause you to walk in my statues, and ye shall keep my judgments, and do them."** That day, while on the turnpike in Breezewood, Pennsylvania, something happened to me. I received a spiritual heart transplant that caused me to want to live my life in a manner pleasing to God.

When God saves us, there is a spiritual transformation that takes place within us. Some people are able to drop old habits immediately and begin to walk in their new way of life. Others may take longer to fully allow the power of God to manifest through their behavior. Do understand that immediate change is very possible. In fact, I'd dare say that it's preferred because, once we are saved, we are free from sin's grip on our lives (Romans 6:14). Though we will still be tempted to sin, the temptation doesn't have to overtake us. **"There hath no temptation taken you but such as is common to man: but God is faithful, who will not suffer you to be tempted above that ye are able; but will with the temptation also make a way to escape, that ye may be able to bear it"** (1 Corinthians 10:13).

People continue to struggle with sin, even after being saved, because there is a war between the flesh and the Spirit of God that dwells within every believer (Galatians 5:17). When the flesh wins, they give in. When the Spirit wins, they are victorious over sin. I was twenty-seven-years old when I finally stopped running and surrendered to God. The stronghold that drugs and alcohol had over me were forever broken. I haven't had a drink since that time nor have I sold or done drugs either. The reason why I know immediate change is possible is because I've experienced it.

Don't simply take my word for it when it comes to changing one's life. I think the Apostle Paul has a story that runs circles around mine. In Acts 7, we learn about Paul, who was referred to as Saul at the time, partaking in the stoning death of Stephen. Stephen was one of the men chosen by the apostles in Acts 6 to help take care of the widows. In verse 8 of Acts 6, he is described as being **"full of faith and power"** who **"did great wonders and miracles among the people."** It's because of his faith that he was martyred and Paul (then called Saul) took pleasure in participating in his death. Paul **"made havock of the church**," in Jerusalem (Acts 8:3). He even sought permission from the high priest to go to the city of Damascus to bring back anyone who was found teaching/believing in Jesus. On his way there, Saul had an encounter with the Lord that forever changed his life (Acts 9:1-6). Instead of a persecutor of Christians, Paul became a preacher of the gospel. Paul lived out the words that he wrote in 2 Corinthians 5:17, **"Therefore if any man be in Christ, he is a new creature: old things are passed away; behold, all things are become new."**

I became a new creature that day I was riding through Pennsylvania. Yes, I had gone to church the previous morning, but my transformation didn't take place at the altar. I don't know why I even went. Maybe I did it because my mom asked me. Perhaps it was because church felt like a "safe" place after the vision I'd seen two nights previously. Or, it could have simply been habitual attendance since I would go on occasion anyhow to shut my parents up. The reason I went escapes me and I don't recall a single word from the sermon. I'm saying all of this to say that one's conversion doesn't have to take place inside the church walls. Pastors give altar calls as they should. (I apparently ignored the one given that Sunday morning.) If God is tugging on your heart, please don't wait until the next time a pastor invites you to the altar to receive the gift of salvation. You can do it now! In the event that you are uncertain about what to say, I have provided a prayer in Appendix A located on page 93 to assist you.

I said "yes" to preaching without having a clue how I was going to go about doing it. I figured I would have to go to school. As I rode back to D.C., I decided to trust God with the details of how everything would come together. I went to work at the car shop and the owner's brother informed me that I'd received an important call from the Dean of

Religious Studies at Howard University. I called and the man said to me, "I understand that you want to study theology, but you don't have a high school diploma." To this day, I have no clue how he obtained my contact information or knew my interests. I'd only recently said yes to God and hadn't had the opportunity to share the things on my heart with anyone. We set up a meeting during which time I told the Dean my story. He arranged things so that I could study for my GED at a local high school during the day and take some theology classes at Howard in the evening. I was on what they called academic probation, but I didn't care. I knew God had answered my prayers with this phone call.

Going to school and continuing working at the shop wasn't an option. Both required much of my time. Yet, I still needed to make money. I shared my struggles with my mother and, once again, she came to my rescue. (There's nothing like having a good mother! Please don't take yours for granted.) Mama bought me a tow truck that I picked up and drove back to D.C. I was able to tow cars and take GED classes during the day. I went to Howard at night.

Nina and I were still a couple when all of this took place, but eventually we broke up. She'd been fussing about my "street" life and all the trouble I was getting into. Yet, when I began to walk in a new direction, that was even harder for her to accept. I tried to bring her into my new world, but she wasn't having it. She liked the me I was before surrendering to God because the new me was boring. I wasn't going out partying, drinking, and drugging, like I'd done previously. I, with all sincerity, wanted to pursue God and that began to bother her.

I was confused by Nina's reaction, but I didn't fight to keep her. I let her go. I guess that was my first time fully understanding that submitting to God meant losing some people close to me. My friends and I no longer had anything in common. "Fast Chili" had turned to "Slow, No Chili." I admit, the abandonment by Nina and other friends hurt, but not enough to turn my back on God. I was willing to lose those relationships if it meant continuing to build one with Him. For those of you who have experienced this type of loss, don't be discouraged. Everyone is not meant to accompany you on your spiritual journey. Whether you're a new Christian or a seasoned one experiencing new levels in your walk with

God, you will have some people who come and go along the way. It's okay. You won't be friendless forever. God will bring people into your life who will help sharpen you (Proverbs 27:17) and He will use you to do the same to someone else.

On a side note, I did see Nina about a decade later. After we'd broken up, she'd gotten strung out on crack and was going through a recovery program. Part of her rehabilitation required her to reach out to me and ask for forgiveness about some things. She did, but she also blamed me for her addiction. She said that if we would have stayed together that she wouldn't have gotten addicted to crack and would have been better off. I didn't understand why I was being blamed, but I didn't argue with her. Breaking up was her decision, not mine. In retrospect, it was a good thing because it allowed me to devote my time to my education and studying the Word of God without any unnecessary drama.

I didn't complete the program at Howard. In 1981, the Lord called me to pastor a church in West Virginia where I ultimately completed coursework for my GED. For the record, when I said "yes" to preaching, I didn't know that pastoring was also in the plan. It's a good thing that God doesn't give us all the details to our assignments when He tells us about them. I had no desire to be a pastor. My father was a pastor. I saw how much he labored and witnessed some of the things he went through with his members. I only wanted to preach, but God had other plans. I'd promised to submit myself to Him. Thus, saying "no" wasn't an option.

Personal Reflections

1. Have you accepted the gift of salvation? If not, and you're ready to do so, please turn to Appendix A on page 93.

2. Being abandoned by friends or loved ones is never a good feeling. What are some ways to cope with such situations without becoming a people-pleaser by submitting to the desire of people over God?

3. Proverbs 27:17 reads, **"Iron sharpeneth iron; so a man sharpeneth the countenance of his friend."** List the name of three friends who spiritually sharpen you. List the name of three friends whom you help to spiritualty sharpen. (It's okay if both lists contain the same names.)

Chapter 6: Ministry, Marriage, & Mayhem

It was in April of 1981 when I took the assignment to temporarily pastor Shiloh Baptist Church in Williamson, West Virginia. Back in my street days, I'd dated a young lady named Diana. Unlike Nina, Diana wasn't into drugs and alcohol. She was what one would call a "good girl." A deacon's daughter, Diana tried to live up to the standards of God and felt that the direction in which I was headed wasn't the way she wanted to go. Thus, Diana and I went our separate ways. After I surrendered my life to Jesus, Diana and I reconnected and started a long distance relationship. Eventually we married. Initially, I was still living in D.C. and she was in Williamson.

When the need for a pastor arose at Shiloh, I accepted the assignment because it allowed me to be closer to my wife. She was a school teacher and the plan was that she would move to D.C. with me after the school year ended. My job was to help the church get on its feet because it had been closed for a while after the previous pastor died. It also had some structural issues. There were three elderly women who loved the church so much that they asked me to help them re-open it and fill in for a short time until they found a permanent pastor. I told them I would.

The church needed a lot of work; much more than what the four of us would have been able to come up with if we had to pay professionals. I was able to connect with some skilled drinking buddies of mine and they hooked a brotha up. We were able to replace the leaking roof on the building and take care of some other cosmetic issues for little to nothing. God had given me favor with them. They were so amazed at my transformation that they were willing to do whatever they could to see that Shiloh was safe to inhabit. My new way of life was a witness to them. Know that when you give your life to Christ, people are watching you. Old friends, enemies, and others should be able to see the difference that Jesus has made in your life without you even saying anything.

My goal was to help Shiloh re-open the church and then return to D.C. with my wife and finish my education. What I thought would be a temporary pastoral assignment, turned into an eight-year appointment. Proverbs 16:9 says, **"A man's heart deviseth his way, but the Lord directeth his steps."** Another Scripture in Proverbs puts it this way, **"There are many devices in a man's heart; nevertheless the counsel of the Lord, that shall stand"** (Proverbs 19:21). The best way to sum up both of these Scriptures is with these words, "Man proposes, God disposes." I don't know who originated this phrase that contains a great truth: We (humans) can make all the plans that we want, but ultimately it will be the will of the Lord that is carried out. He will be the sole determiner of whether or not our plans fail or succeed. A lot of our frustration comes from wanting to do things in our own power instead of by His. He gives us that choice. He allows us to obey Him or rebel against Him. I could have stuck to my plan to return to D.C., but then I would have missed out on the blessing of being used by God to build Shiloh Baptist Church from three members to over fifty in a matter of a few months.

Shiloh continued to grow rapidly. Things were moving so fast that it was unreal. I still had my tow truck and continued towing cars on the side to make money. It was my personal finances and those of others that helped fund the church. The ministry grew tremendously in size. More than the number, I'm amazed by the types of people that the Lord drew to the church. Unlike most of today's churches that are filled with folks who act like they were morally good sinners (as if that makes a difference when it comes to salvation), the majority of the members at Shiloh were varying degrees of recovering addicts. Shiloh was the spiritual hospital where the sick came to be healed and delivered. It was such a blessing to witness. Sure, we had some people who continued to struggle, but most of those who attended had been delivered and it showed through their worship.

I know some preachers say that once a person is delivered from crack that they don't need to go back to the crack house to try and witness because they will only end up falling into temptation. This is true. What is equally true is that it depends on the person and how much he/she allows God to lead and work in and through them. I don't suggest that anyone goes anywhere unless God says so. If He does, then you should be obedient and not allow fear to stop you. There's no way that I could have witnessed to recovering alcoholics in my own strength. I liked alcohol too much when I was in the world. If I would have gone to Shiloh outside of God's will and on my own, the power of God would not have been manifested through me there. Perhaps, I would have regressed. I don't know and, quite frankly, it's a moot point because I know for a fact that God led me there. I would not have been able to do anything in my own power. It's only by the power of God working through me that I was able to be around people, some of whom I used to be like, and not falter in my walk with God, but rather help them along on their journey. The point to take away from this is if whatever you're doing is having a positive, spiritual impact on the lives of others, please don't think it's you doing the work. It's God working through you. He, alone, should get the glory.

In Luke 7, when Simon, a Pharisee, observed the woman who washed Jesus's feet with her tears, dried them with her hair, kissed, and poured oil on them, he silently questioned Jesus's discernment, saying to himself, **"This man, if he were a prophet, would have known who and what manner of woman this is that toucheth him: for she is a sinner"** (Luke 7:39). Jesus's response in Luke 7:47 was to acknowledge that the woman had many sins which had been forgiven. Because of the forgiveness of her numerous sins, she loved Him much. There's nothing like seeing a crowd of changed believers worshiping God collectively on a regular basis. These are people whose praise was unrestricted. They had been forgiven of much and their abundant love for Jesus was demonstrated through their uninhibited actions.

I'm quite certain that we consistently violated fire safety codes at Shiloh. The inside of that church would be filled to capacity and then some. It was a two-story building and, at times, there would be so many people at service that folks downstairs could see the floor shaking upstairs. Talk about excitement and nervousness all at the same time! I appreciated that people enjoyed coming, but Lord knows I was concerned about the possibility of someone falling through the floor. Thankfully, the Lord heard my plea. We never had any such casualties. I stayed with Shiloh until the spring of 1989 when I accepted a pastoral assignment in White Sulphur Springs, West Virginia. Before I move on to the miraculous works that took place there, there are some important things that happened between 1981 and 1989 that are worth mentioning.

My marriage began experiencing turmoil almost immediately after I started pastoring. I don't know why Diana married me, but I didn't have the purest motives when I married her. Diana was a school teacher and she was smart. I thought being with her would be beneficial because she could help me improve my literary skills. I was a man without a high school diploma (at the time we married) who had caught the attention of an educated woman. I wasn't the best speller and my lack of education made me insecure. The solution to fix my insecurity was to hook up with Diana who, I thought, would make me feel better about myself.

Where was God in all of this? Good question. I don't recall consulting Him and, if I did, I didn't clearly hear what He had to say. Marriage is a sacred institution that He created to be between one man and one woman for life (Genesis 2:24). I loved Diana. My love for her should have been the primary motive for marrying her, but it was secondary. The intent was for her to help better me. I didn't value her the way I should have as her husband and, as the years went by, it showed.

Insecurity is a dangerous thing. A lot of times when we're exposed to our own shortcomings, we try quick fixes that really aren't solutions at all. Rather, they are cover-ups to deeper issues that still remain once our human remedy wears off. Take, for example, a young girl who feels unloved by her father. She may look for this validation in relationships with other men. That may work for a while, but soon she will see their flaws or they'll see hers, and the deep need still remains unfulfilled. It's important that we look to and depend on God to address all of the issues in our lives. We have a tendency to go to Him for certain things and try to handle others on our own. I thought that marrying Diana was what God would have me to do because, if I was educated, it would better my service to Him. At least that was the lie I told myself.

Even to this day, I am a firm believer in preachers being educated, but man's seal of approval is not a prerequisite in order to be used by God. I felt insecure because most of the other preachers I knew had been "properly" trained. Here I was, a high school dropout who'd reconnected with an intelligent woman. Diana had a brand new Monte Carlo. All I had was my tow truck. My own feelings of inadequacy are what caused me to try and manipulate the benefits of being married to Diana. Once again, my plans backfired. My school-teacher wife didn't teach me a single thing! It's not her fault that she didn't live up to my expectations. It was unfair of me to put them on her.

Diana could sing and play the piano, so she helped with the choir. Doing so was out of her comfort zone because, unlike me, Diana wasn't a people person. She actually came across as a bit standoffish to others. It didn't help matters in our marriage when I was transporting members and their children in her brand new car. Like I said, Shiloh was comprised of a lot of marginalized people who didn't necessarily have means of transportation. Her Monte Carlo wasn't big, but I would squeeze as many folks as I could into it and take them to and from church. Diana wasn't feeling that at all. I didn't understand why she couldn't join in my enthusiasm about the fact that these people were coming to church. She didn't understand why I had to be so hands-on and involved in everyone's life.

In 1982, Diana had a miscarriage for which she blamed me. She said that if I wasn't pushing her to do so much with the church then she would not have lost the baby. I challenged her on that point. We had a church full of recovering addicts who had popped out babies left and right. Surely, Diana had taken better care of her body than they had. The miscarriage created even more tension in our marriage. Like many couples, we didn't stop to address the root of our issues. We kept functioning in the midst of our dysfunction.

The next time Diana got pregnant was in 1983 and she was determined not to make the same "mistakes" as she had previously. For nearly the entire duration of her pregnancy, Diana did not attend church or participate in helping with ministry in any manner. That was rough on our marriage and on me personally. I was a pastor without the support of my wife. It would have been different if her decision had been prescribed by her obstetrician. It wasn't. I know Diana felt like she was doing what was best for our child, so I can't fault her for having her heart in the right place. Her head, on the other hand, was on another planet. Nevertheless, in the end, Diana gave birth to our beautiful baby girl, Kristen, in 1984.

After Kristen was born, the personal relationship between Diana and me didn't improve. We continued to coexist without connecting. In the spring of 1989, an opportunity to preach at a church about three hours away in White Sulphur Springs, West Virginia was presented. One of the reasons I decided to take it was because it provided more financial stability for my family. Diana's teaching salary was our family's only stable income. I wasn't getting paid much, if anything, from the church and the towing business had its ups and downs. Diana and I discussed this move and the plan was for her to relocate once the school year ended.

In June, Diana and Kristen, who was five at the time, moved from Williamson to White Sulphur Springs. We put the house up for sale and sold all of the furniture. I'd already been living in our new furnished home. Diana intended to get a teaching job in the local school district, but she didn't get in. She felt that she had too much experience and time under her belt to be a substitute and wanted to move back to Williamson. Consequently, the house was taken off of the market, re-furnished, and she and Kristen left.

I was in a new place in a new pastoral position, which I was sure that God had blessed me with, and yet I was experiencing personal defeat. Diana and I tried commuting for the first two years, but the circumstances did not help our already strained relationship. Our marital issues never displayed themselves externally. We were publicly close and privately distant. That distance would permanently be sealed when Diana made the decision to file for divorce.

Personal Reflections

1. Keep in mind that whether you're saved or unsaved, God has the right to determine what will and what will not work out in your life. Read Proverbs 16:9 and 19:21. What plans have you had for your own life that have been overruled by God's?

2. What insecurities do you have that you've tried to fix yourself? What was the end result? Were your efforts a permanent solution to your issues?

3. We often present others with a skewed view about the reality of our lives. What are some things you're currently experiencing that others would be surprised to know?

Chapter 7: Feelings & Frustrations

Unfortunately, we live in a world where "for better or worse" or "'til death do us apart," really means "'til I can't take it anymore" or "'til you do something that gets on my last nerves." We have the-straw-that-broke-the-camel's-back syndrome. No matter what kind of spin we try to put on things to justify our own actions, the Bible is clear that God hates divorce (Malachi 2:16).

Divorce goes against God's original design for marriage. It tears families apart, especially when there are children involved. There are only two instances under which God allows divorce, according to the Bible. One scenario is for sexual immorality (Matthew 5:32; 19:9), and the other is when a husband or wife has abandoned his/her spouse (1 Corinthians 7:15). Even under these circumstances, divorce isn't a requirement. Reconciliation is possible though it will take a lot of work from both parties. Nonetheless, anyone who divorces under such circumstances has biblical grounds to do so.

We also have a whole nation of people who divorce for various other reasons. How often have you heard someone say of his/her spouse, "He/she is no longer the person I married?" What they are really saying is that there are qualities about this person's character that either they overlooked previously or didn't see. Either way, something about their spouse has become undesirable, or perhaps even unbearable in that person's opinion. When we focus on the negative qualities of our spouses, those things become magnified in our minds and overshadow any good characteristics he/she may have. Soon, the idea that life would be much better if we weren't married to this person becomes increasingly appealing and then we're off to divorce court.

The church is called to be a light unto the world (Matthew 5:14). However, when we mistreat the institution of marriage, we're not portraying the kind of relationship that God originally intended. When asked about divorce, Jesus said, "**Moses because of the hardness of your hearts suffered** you to put away your wives: but from the beginning it was not so" (Matthew 19:8). Marriage is a sacred institution between one man and one woman (Genesis 2:24; Matthew 19:5-6). I believe the church is at fault for some of the marriage battles taking place across our country now. People see same-sex "marriage" as no big deal because we have made a mockery of our vows, especially Christians. It's hard to be a shining light to the world for marriage when we have so much mess occurring in our own marriages. Make no mistake about it, no marriage is perfect, but all marriages can be continually perfected through Christ. No matter how we try to skirt around the issue, Jesus says that the provision of divorce was made because of the hardness of hearts. We have disgraced the institution of marriage and have taken it for granted. As a result, we're now seeing the consequences of our actions.

When my parents got divorced, I was extremely judgmental of my daddy. He was a pastor and, though I wasn't walking with the Lord, I was still against pastors getting divorced. After I got married and became a pastor myself, I was even harsher on divorcing from the pulpit. I lacked compassion for others. Yet, I yearned for such when Diana and I were going through our divorce. I felt convicted. Torn. I said that divorce was something I would never do. When it happened, I was forced to eat a huge piece of humble pie. I was being met with the same measure of judgment that I'd given out and it felt horrible.

Just because I went through this experience, it doesn't mean that my view on divorce has changed. My views can't change because God's Word doesn't. He still hates divorce. I felt so strongly against divorce that I can say with certainty I would still be married to Diana to this day had she not left me. I didn't divorce her. She divorced me. As I look back at my own actions, perhaps I made her feel like she had no choice. I was more committed to the bride of Christ (the church) than I was to my own bride. Our biggest arguments were about church. In the previous chapter, I mentioned that I married Diana for all the wrong reasons. That still doesn't change the fact that we were married. I was not as attentive to her as I should have been . . . as I needed to be. I complained about her not wanting me to transport people in her car. Maybe that was her simply wanting my time to herself because it was something she never got much of. I don't know. I do know that I failed her. I can make up all the excuses in the world, but the bottom line is that I take full responsibility for the demise of my first marriage. This is not to say that Diana was perfect. Yes, she had her faults, but God created a divine order. My allegiance should have first been to Him, to Diana, and then to the church. Instead, my priorities were God, the church, some more church, church again, and then Diana.

I was so happy about how God was moving at Shiloh that I thought I was doing right at the time. It's only in hindsight that I see the error of my ways. I wonder if Diana was standoffish because my actions caused her to resent the church. Only God knows what would have happened if I had placed Diana in her proper position in my life. Maybe we would have seen even greater works at Shiloh. Maybe she and Kristen would have stayed in White Sulphur Springs after we moved there. There's a lot of would haves, could haves, and should haves, but I don't look back. The Lord has graciously blessed me with my current wife, Brenda, to whom I've been married for over twenty years.

Perhaps you're struggling in your marriage right now and think, "See, things worked out for you. I'll divorce my spouse and take the lessons I learn from this experience and apply them to my next marriage when God blesses me with another spouse." First of all, God doesn't need us to create opportunities for Him to bless us. Please don't leave your husband/wife and think that things will be better the next time. They could be worse. I did learn from my first marriage and I have done much better this time around, but it doesn't mean that Brenda and I haven't gone through some things. We have. I wasn't looking to re-marry. It happened and I have been blessed. I can't even say that I regret how things turned out between Diana and me. To do that would be an insult to my wife whom I dearly love. There's not a bone in me that would ever wish away our twenty-year plus history. My point for sharing is for everyone out there to understand that God hates divorce! It is possible, with God's help, to work out the issues in your marriage.

Everyone please take note. If your ministry or job is coming between you and your spouse, ask God to help you to re-prioritize! If you don't think you need to re-prioritize, pray for direction anyhow. Your first ministry is at home. God didn't bless you with whatever gift you have for it to cause division between you and your spouse. Despite the lie that some people tell, God is not going to tell you to divorce your husband/wife so that you can be free to do more ministry. In case you didn't catch it the first few times I wrote the statement, let me do it once more... *God hates divorce!*

If you are divorced, please don't walk around with your head hung low in shame. You can't undo the past. Learn from it, grow from it, and become better because of it. If you're struggling in your marriage and are considering divorce, don't give up! Maybe your spouse has committed adultery or has abandoned you and so you feel justified in divorcing that person. You are correct. You do have the right to do so. Before making that decision, I want you to ask yourself a few questions.

1. Have you given God a chance to heal your heart? Healing has to take place whether or not the divorce goes through. In a broken state, a writ of divorcement won't fix your pain. As a matter of fact, it can increase it because of the added emotional stress that comes along with divorce. Allowing God to heal you may give you a new perspective of the problems you and your spouse face.

2. Is your decision a result of anger or unforgiveness toward your spouse? A husband or wife who truly repents of his/her wrongs is different from one who doesn't. Have you rejected your spouse's sincere pleas for forgiveness? Whether or not that person apologizes, forgiveness is still necessary. It's also a crucial aspect of your healing process.

3. What are you hoping the divorce will accomplish? Do you think it will bring you peace? A new, better relationship with someone else? Only you and God know whether there are any ulterior motives for wanting to divorce your mate. If you don't come clean to anyone else, be honest with Him.

Pastors and their families often live our lives in fish tanks. All eyes are on us. I know there were congregants watching me, both at Shiloh and at First Baptist in White Sulphur Springs. I wish I could have shown them a better example of a husband. I hate to think that my divorce could have been a stumbling block to someone else's marriage. What hope does the congregation have if the leaders of the church can't keep their marriages together? What hope does the world have that God's definition of marriage is how it should be if the church fails to live out His original blueprint for this union?

Personal Reflections

1. What's your view about divorce? Is it the same as God's?

2. Have you gone through a divorce? What are some of the things you could have done differently in your marriage?

3. Read Luke 6:36-38. Is there a situation in which you have harshly judged others and then found yourself in the same position?

Chapter 8: Covered by Grace

I've found that one of the most frustrating things in ministry is to continuously give out love to others and not receive it back. When Diana and I were married, I struggled with her coldness. It was hard coming home after doing "God's work" and not receiving emotional support from my wife. Again, as mentioned in Chapter 7, I take responsibility for the failing of our marriage. I, the head of the household, neglected my wife. Ultimately, the responsibility lies on my shoulder according to the biblical order of things (1 Corinthians 11:3; Ephesians 5:25-28).

This wisdom I now have regarding my first marriage is after the fact. At the time, I was simply frustrated by how distant Diana and I had become. We had gotten to a place of coexisting without cooperating. We were neither emotionally nor physically intimate with one another. Consequently, there was a lot of temptation.

If those who are happily married can be tempted, then it should be no surprise that miserable couples face this issue as well. The enemy comes to steal, kill, and destroy (John 10:10). He doesn't want anything that God does to or through us to prosper. Marriage is no exception. Evidence of the enemy's attack on marriage can be found through the increased divorce rate, advocacy of those attempting to re-define marriage as anything other than between one man and woman, and the issues that abound within this institution of couples who remain married without experiencing the joy of their union. Unhappy couples may not divorce for whatever reason, but they are still being stripped of enjoying marriage to its fullest.

While Diana and I lived as husband and wife, I found strength in the Lord to resist any temptation that came my way. No matter what the situation, I was her husband and I'd refused to violate our vows. Once we went our separate ways, I gave into the lusts of my flesh. I was preaching righteousness and practicing unrighteousness with women outside of the pulpit. The struggle of being saved and single is real. Sex is a legitimate need and a beautiful mechanism that God has given us to take pleasure in with each other. We defile this gift when it is used outside of His parameters. That is, outside of the marital relationship between a husband and a wife.

You may be wondering why the dynamics of a relationship matter when it comes to sex if there are two consenting adults involved. Simply put, it matters because it violates God's divine order of things. A more extensive answer would involve a discussion of the emotional, physical, and spiritual consequences of sex outside of marriage. Emotionally, feelings get involved. In a marital relationship, this is a good thing. A wife should be emotionally wrapped up in her husband and vice versa. There's an investment in the relationship and one party will not be made to feel like he/she is just a "booty call." Sex is rewarding within the marital relationship in many ways. Those who have sex without getting their emotions involved are really missing out on all that sex has to offer. They are cheating themselves of the ultimate sexual experience. I did that when I had sex with women whom I knew I wouldn't marry. They began to develop feelings for me that were not reciprocated. The end result was a lot of unnecessary drama.

The spiritual consequences of sex outside of the marital relationship can best be explained by Paul's words in 1 Corinthians 6:15-20, **"Know ye not that your bodies are the members of Christ? shall I then take the members of Christ, and make them the members of an harlot? God forbid. What? know ye not that he which is joined to an harlot is one body? for two, saith he, shall be one flesh. But he that is joined unto the Lord is one spirit. Flee fornication. Every sin that a man doeth is without the body; but he that committeth fornication sinneth against his own body. What? know ye not that your body is the temple of the Holy Ghost which is in you, which ye have of God, and ye are not your own? For ye are bought with a price: therefore glorify God in your body, and in your spirit, which are God's."** If the Spirit of God dwells in you, then your body is the temple of God. Don't willingly defile your temple for a few moments of pleasure. It's not worth the guilt, the stress of worrying about an unplanned pregnancy, the paranoia of whether or not you gave someone an STD (or contracted one), and it's certainly not worth the grief that we cause God.

It's normal to feel lonely or have sexual desires. People have a tendency to see preachers as superhuman. They don't expect us to have the same struggles as they do because they seem to think that our position immunizes us from life's daily trials. At the same time, some preachers use humanness to make excuses for their sins. Neither approach is correct. Yes, we are human and capable of succumbing to the same desires as anyone else. Yet, our leadership position should make us want to uphold the standards of God to the utmost (Luke 12:47-48; James 3:1). This is not to say that, if I wasn't a pastor or in some type of leadership position, fornicating would have been okay. As a matter of fact, in 1 Corinthian 5, Paul admonishes the church for their sexual immorality. Similar to how I neglected to fully perform all of my duties as a husband when Diana and I were married, I also failed to live up to the true standards of a pastor. In each instance, God used me in spite of me to bless the congregations I was serving.

Of course, the congregants didn't know what I was doing. At least I don't think they did. The thing about sin is, even when we try to keep our doings a secret, it can be exposed. Though I didn't mess around with any women in my congregation, I don't know who knew whom and what conversations happened behind my back. If you're a pastor or in another type of leadership position in your church and you're sleeping around with members of your congregation, *stop it!* It is impossible to lead people with whom you are sexually and immorally involved. If you're not in a leadership position and you're sleeping around with members of your congregation, *stop it!* You may not be leading anyone, but you certainly are hindering their walk with Christ. If you're a Christian and you are sleeping with one or many people within your congregation or without, *stop it!*

Be it preacher or layman, we are all called to **"flee fornication"** (1 Corinthians 6:18). Because it is natural to desire sex, we cannot depend on our own strength to help us resist temptation. If we tell others that God can deliver them from anything, then we must also trust Him to deliver us from ourselves.

I created many unnecessary issues in my life during that time period as a result of my actions. I almost missed the blessing of meeting and marrying

Brenda because I was consumed with women troubles. I was dating a lady in Louisiana and another in Virginia. I'd visit them and we'd go to the movies, out to dinner, and involve ourselves in ungodly recreation. (Use your unsanctified imagination to put the rest of the meat on the bones.) It got to a point where they both wanted more and I didn't want much from either of them except the companionship.

I strongly urge any single man, especially if you're a pastor, to avoid close friendships with females with whom you have no intention of marrying. Again, married folks struggle with temptation. At the end of the day, hopefully, they have their wives to go home to and fulfill their sexual needs in a legitimate manner. A single man has nothing but temptation with which to deal. It's difficult, but it is possible to rise above the lusts of your flesh. A single pastor's major focus should be on his relationship with God and his ministry. A single man's major focus should be on his relationship with God and ways in which he can serve in whatever ministry God has for him. (The same goes for single females.) Occupy your mind with something fruitful. Keep a Scripture or two handy for quick recall when tempted. I wish I had put these mechanisms in place after things went south between Diana and me. I would have saved myself a lot of headaches.

Through all the things I've been through, even things brought upon myself, I've learned to depend on God. Though I knew I was doing wrong by messing around with the women, I also knew that they were not marriage material and so I refused to take that leap. My flesh was out of control. I could have easily dropped one of them and married the other in efforts to legitimize what we were doing. Feeling convicted about my behavior, I tried to end things, but I had irrational, emotional women on my hands. See, sin has a way of taking you through more than you want to experience. When I wanted to stop, I couldn't. It became easier to appease them through a physical relationship than to break things off and deal with the potential fallout. I felt trapped. Had I been doing things the way that God intended, I would have never been in this situation.

The bottom line is that one must always seek God's desire for his/her destiny. Be it in marriage, ministry, schooling, or any other aspect of your life, trust the Lord to order your steps. Ask the Lord to help you desire the design that He has for your life. This is something that I've learned to do regularly. When we desire what it is that God wants for us, we never have to worry about whether or not it is the right thing. Whatever God has in store for us is the best. If you have messed up in any manner, know that God's grace can cover you. We shouldn't take advantage of His grace (Romans 6:1-2), rather accept it, be thankful for it, and be freed from the grip of sin by it.

Personal Reflections

1. In 1 Corinthians 5, Paul outlines the discipline that should be taken against those involved in sexual immorality. Why do you think that many pastors avoid addressing this issue nowadays?

2. What are some other ways in which we defile our temples besides sexual immorality?

3. God has a divine destiny for your life though He will not give you all of the details up front. Are you willing to relinquish control over your own life and trust Him to lead you? If yes, what things must you give up or stop doing? If no, what is stopping you?

Chapter 9: A Second Chance for Love

The first time my wife, Brenda, and I met was in June of 1994 in Richmond, Virginia. I was a guest lecturer at the National Baptist Congress of Christian Education for a dear friend of mine who was in charge of the youth department. The National Baptist Congress of Christian Education is a week-long event with the sole purpose of building up various ministries within the church via collective training.[4] My friend taught adults how to build up the youth ministries in their churches. He'd invited me to speak to his class because he knew how well things were going with the youth ministry at First Baptist. He also said to me, "your wife is in my class." Much like Sarah did when the angel said that she would have a son, I laughed (Genesis 18:10-12). Without disclosing the details of my indiscretions, I said that my plate was too full to even consider the thought of marrying again.

Our mutual friend was quite persistent and introduced us anyway. Brenda was beautiful. She reminded me of the character Whitley Gilbert on *A Different World* played by actress Jasmine Guy. Pretty or not, I wasn't interested in pursuing a relationship with Brenda or anyone else. I was trying to get out of the mess I was already in with women. Still, at our relentless friend's insistence, we exchanged numbers before leaving town.

Neither of us called the other. I was so adamant about not getting involved with anyone that, in August, when I saw this friend again and he asked me about her, I didn't know whom he was speaking about. He jogged my memory by repeating his previous statement about her being my wife. Again, I rebuked him, but he wouldn't take no for an answer. He knew about an upcoming trip I had to New Orleans for a convention and that I would be stopping through Memphis, Tennessee where Brenda lived. He asked me if I would at least reach out to her. I agreed to do so.

I think a large part of my agreeing to contact Brenda was to shut our friend up. Despite the fact that I'd had a dream about marrying a woman years prior, I didn't get excited when this man said that Brenda was to be my wife. I knew him very well. He was a dynamic man of God. He wasn't one of those who would prophe*lie* for publicity or to gain someone's approval. He was sincere in his walk with God and all that he was called to do. Still, I didn't give his words any weight. I'd already prematurely jumped into one marriage. That was of my own doing. There was no way I would let someone force me into another. I knew enough to know that, if my friend was speaking prophetically, God would confirm things to me somehow. Since I wasn't looking for a wife, there was nothing for God to confirm. At least that's what I thought. I would soon learn that this was another case of "man proposes, God disposes" that I mentioned in Chapter 6 when referencing Proverbs 16:9 and 19:21.

A week or so before I was to leave for New Orleans, I contacted Brenda to see if she would be interested in meeting when I came through her town. She remembered me from our June encounter and said yes. On the way to the convention, I called her from my cell phone when I got to Memphis. This was the day before fancy touch-screen and compact phones. I had a big, bulky phone that was mounted to the car floor. (Isn't it amazing how technology has changed?) Anyhow, Brenda informed me that she'd recently been released from the emergency room where she had been treated for food poisoning. She stated that she would still like to meet with me anyway. We met at Denny's and had a wonderful conversation. I followed her home and stayed about a half hour or so before getting back on the road.

Brenda and I spoke on the phone every night while I was in Louisiana. I didn't know it at the time, but a relationship was budding between us. On the way back home, I stopped in Memphis and we, again, hooked up at a restaurant. We met in the parking lot and, as we were walking into the building, I saw her reflection in the glass and it freaked me out. She looked exactly like the woman I'd seen in a dream. In it, the Lord told me that this woman would be my wife. Of course, I dismissed it as simply a dream then. I don't know why I wasn't reminded of this when Brenda and I saw each other for the first time in Richmond, Virginia. Perhaps, it was because I'd been so adamant about not wanting to re-marry that my mind was closed to any possibility. After sitting down and talking to her the first time, I had become smitten.

Brenda wasn't only physically beautiful. Her spirit was as well. (Still is to this day!) I admired her tenacity. She was a single, God-fearing mother of two who did not let life's circumstances stop her from being successful. At the risk of sounding crazy, I told Brenda about the dream and the trouble I was having with the other women as a result of my rebelliousness. I spilled all the beans right there outside of the restaurant. I gave her enough information to easily run her off. If she thought I was crazy, she was kind enough not to tell me. She listened without judgment or fear about me saying that I believed she was my wife. She didn't say much. In fact, I'm not sure if she said anything. We went inside the restaurant, had a good meal, and then I left to return to West Virginia.

After that visit, Brenda and I stayed in touch. I would drive to see her about once a month. In the midst of my traveling, I still preached every Sunday and was back in time for Wednesday night service. We kept our encounters pure. I never stayed overnight at her house; I always booked a hotel. Miraculously, the trouble I had with the other women dissipated. I don't know how I was finally able to shake them, but I did. Brenda was the only one on whom my desire was set. Sometimes she would question my love and I'd tell her to think about all the driving I was doing. It was about a seven hundred mile trip each way! Even with gas prices much lower back then, I was still investing a lot of time and money simply to lay eyes on her.

I think about the circumstances with Brenda and I am thankful to God for a second chance. I don't know why He chose to have favor on me, especially because I wasn't living as I should have been as a pastor. His grace covered me and there was nothing I did to deserve it. His grace covers you in all of your failures as well, be it your marriage, sinful behavior, or anything else. We have to surrender to Him in all of our ways and that includes whether or not to marry.

If you're not looking to marry and the Lord really does bring someone into your life, listen. You should also be willing to walk away from a relationship if He says so. For the record, I don't mean walking away from your marriage. I think I pretty much summed up how God feels about marriage in the last chapter. In any event, when it comes to marrying (or anything that God has for you) don't let people talk you into something.

Though our friend said that Brenda and I were "meant to be," it wasn't his voice that I submitted to. It was God's. Had I continued my stubbornness, there's no telling what kind of mess I would be in this very day. I proposed to Brenda on February 14, 1995. We were married on April 29 of that same year and she has been my bride ever since.

Personal Reflections

1. Do you remember when you met your significant other/spouse? Is there anything special that stands out about that day?

2. Has God ever spoken to you in a dream? Reflect on that experience.

3. Name some instances when your foolishness was covered by God's grace.

Chapter 10: The Good, the Bad, & the Ugly of Blended Families

I resigned as pastor of First Baptist and moved to Memphis, Tennessee to marry and be with Brenda. If you recall, Diana and I had tried commuting and it didn't work out too well in the end. I didn't want to begin a new marriage by implementing a technique that had failed in my first one. Plus, let's just say that I was eager to share a bed each night with this beautiful woman with whom the Lord had blessed me. There's no need to go into detail. I'm sure you can put the pieces of the puzzle together.

Brenda would have come to White Sulphur Springs, West Virginia where I was, but there were a lot of factors involved. For starters, she had two daughters. Ashley was a few months older than my daughter, Kristen. They were both ten at the time. Brenda's youngest, Brittany, was around eight. Brenda, a preacher's daughter, understood the responsibilities that were on my shoulders as the pastor of First Baptist. She was more than willing to join my side in White Sulphur Springs, but ultimately, I thought it was best for everyone if I moved. I didn't think it would be fair to uproot her girls from the only home that they'd ever known and send them into culture shock.

There's a huge cultural difference between Memphis, Tennessee and White Sulphur Springs, West Virginia. Other than the one five-star hotel, there was nothing much attraction wise there back then. (I'm not sure if that has changed now.) Those who grew up in White Sulphur Springs were likely used to the lack of extracurricular activities. For two girls born and raised in Memphis, it would have been the equivalent of a prison sentence.

Also factoring into my decision to move was Brenda's job. She worked as a team leader for an insurance company that required her to travel to various parts of the United States to meet with business executives and acquire new contracts. It was a good position and I knew she wouldn't be able to find that caliber of employment in White Sulphur Springs.

Recalling the stress that Diana went through to find a job when she moved from Williamson to join me in, I didn't want to add that same burden to Brenda. I didn't want her to make sacrifices that she could possibly resent me for later. So, with thirty-five hundred dollars in my pocket, my car, and other belongings, I moved west with God on my side.

The one thing that did hurt me was knowing that I would be even further away from Kristen. We hadn't lived in the same city since she was about five, but at least we had been in the same state. Not so when I went to Memphis. Diana agreed to let Kristen come to Tennessee for the summer and also during school breaks. Eventually all worked out. I enrolled in Crichton College in Memphis, hoping to finish my education. I also sent out some resumes and, in less than a year, New Jerusalem Missionary Baptist Church brought me in as their new pastor.

Overall, the move had gone well, but there was some trouble stirring within our newly-formed family. Our daughters all got along great. Spiritually, I adopted Brenda's two girls as if they were my own. I have always believed that, if a man married a woman with children, he had to be willing to accept those children and take responsibility for them as if they'd come from his loins. (Vice versa for a woman who marries a man with children.) I did exactly that with Ashley and Brittany.

To be totally transparent, I hate the terms stepparent or stepchild. To this day, I do not refer to Brenda's girls as my stepdaughters. They are my daughters. Case closed! It doesn't matter that their biological father is still in the picture. I didn't come in trying to replace him. I came into the marriage with the intent of not making a difference between them and Kristen. However, I'm not convinced that my wife took on the same mentality as I did.

Brenda, no doubt, loved and accepted Kristen, but their relationship was like that of oil and water initially. I was stuck in the middle, hearing it from both ends. It was difficult because I loved both of them and wanted them to, at least, like each other. I tried not to intervene because there was no malicious intent from either of them at the root of their conflict. They had personality differences that lasted well throughout Kristen's high school years. Eventually, Brenda and Kristen were able to get to a point of cordial exchanges and, ultimately, a loving relationship. In fact, years later when Kristen gave birth to my grandson, Brenda was with her in the delivery room.

The reality of being a "blended family" didn't hit me until after an argument that Brenda and I had one day. Kristen had finished her fourth tour in the service and was staying with us. There was some tension between them, but nothing serious as far as I was concerned. Yet, Brenda made the comment to me that two grown women couldn't live in the same house. The implication was that Kristen would have to leave. I flipped. Ashley and Brittany were grown and had only recently moved out. We'd made allowances for them to stay with us. I thought it would only be fair for us to do the same for Kristen. It became a "your daughters" versus "my daughter" exchange and that hurt me to my core. To me, they were all "our daughters." Brenda made the comment that, at the end of the day, we were a blended family. She was right, but I didn't want to accept or even admit that. Later, when Brenda got sick, the reality of our family dynamics once again hit me in the face.

For anyone who finds yourself in a blended family situation where there's conflict between your child and spouse, the first thing I would suggest is to remain neutral as much as you can. Of course, if someone is doing something egregiously wrong, then you must step in. Do so by addressing the issue and not attacking the person. The change can be traumatic for your spouse and child. In Kristen's case, she was going from being the only child to the middle of three. Though she and her sisters got along then, and still do to this day, I'm sure that could have played a role in her emotions. For Brenda, she had to mother a child whom she had no hand in raising for the first ten years of Kristen's life. There were likely things that Brenda would have taught, or perhaps, not have taught Kristen if she'd been involved in her formidable years. That was a lot of adjusting on both parts. If you're the person in the middle, you have to be compassionate to both your child and your spouse. Never let one mistreat the other. Demand respect from them both, for yourself and for each other.

If you're the stepparent or stepchild whose bumping heads with the other, try to put your differences aside and get along for the sake of your loved one. He/she loves you both and it hurts to love two people who can't find a way to also love each other. Instead of focusing on the negative attributes about your stepparent or stepchild, it would help if you direct your focus on the good things about that individual. If you're thinking that he/she doesn't have any positive attributes, then ask the Lord to help you find some. The bottom line is that you're family. Blood or not, you're family.

It may have taken Brenda a while to get stepparenting down, but she was on top of things as a wife was concerned. Particularly so as a pastor's wife. I'm not purposely trying to compare my wives, but there was a hundred percent difference in the support I received from Brenda and the support from Diana. I'd grown up a lot, too. I knew to involve my wife in decision-making and to make sure she knew that she was a priority. Like I said before, Brenda was a preacher's kid, so she was already aware of what it took to pastor a church. She understood my duties and I'm proud to say that she was indeed my **"help meet"** as God said of Eve in reference to Adam (Genesis 2:18).

A lot of women want to be a pastor's wife because they are drawn to the lure and image of being the "First Lady" of a church. They fail to understand the cost of going into ministry. It comes with a price tag. It's a price that the pastor, his wife, and their children all have to pay in terms of time, money, and sharing of themselves with others. In addition, a pastor's wife must be secure in herself. It's sad to say, but some women are shameless when it comes to throwing themselves at a pastor. He has to be a man of integrity and resist the temptation. He must shut it down immediately. A man, pastor or not, should not entertain conversations with any females that pose a threat to his marriage, even if such threat seems benign. (The same goes for women when it comes to men.) In reality, the devil doesn't care if you view someone's flirtatious behavior or inappropriate comments as harmless. I'm sure he'd prefer that you do. It's easier for him to blind you that way. Do all you can to keep any potential threats away from your marriage. Don't give the enemy a foothold. As the old folks used to day, "Don't let the devil ride. If you let him ride, he'll wanna drive."

In the grand scheme of life, everyone has some kind of insecurities. Brenda included. However, her confidence outweighed any issues she had. I loved the way she carried herself. She knew she was bad and I liked that about her. Brenda would have women come up to her and make innuendos about being able to take me from her and she would look at them like, "try it if you want to make a fool of yourself." Physically speaking, that was an attractive attribute to me. Sometimes I'd be required to be out late to counsel this person or visit so-and-so who was on the sick and shut-in list. My wife knew there was no danger lurking in the waters in terms of my fidelity. I appreciated that. We, as pastors, give a lot of ourselves. We have to constantly show love to members of our congregation. We're a father-figure to children without fathers in their lives. We're the male guidance to females without husbands. It can be tiring to give of yourself day in and day out. I admit that sometimes, when I came home, I was all talked out. I thank my wife so much for being supportive and understanding.

When it comes to a pastor having to choose between his family and the church, his family is definitely first according to Scripture (1 Timothy 5:8). It takes a lot of prayer to keep the balance. To this very day, God helps me prioritize my time. I firmly believe that it's necessary for a pastor, and anyone in ministry or not, to have separate time for his wife and children apart from church. Even if the children aren't biologically his, it is still essential to spend time with them. A blended family was never in God's original design for the family. Sometimes we find ourselves in this situation because of abandonment or death of a parent. Far more often, it's a result of a broken relationship. Families, in general, have their problems. There's added stress of trying to merge individuals together who have no innate connection with one another. Though peace may seem like an impossibility, know that nothing is impossible with God.

Personal Reflections

1. Do you currently have or were you raised in a blended family? If yes, what were the circumstances that created such?

2. What are some challenges faced with your blended family? If your family is running smoothly, what are some things you think helped keep things peaceful?

3. Do you agree with the following statement, "A blended family was never in God's original design for the family?" Why or why not?

Chapter 11: In Sickness & in Health

I pastored in Memphis, Tennessee from the end of 1995 until the spring of 2009 when Brenda and I moved to Sandusky, Ohio so that I could lead Ebenezer Baptist Church there. This is the church where I currently pastor and is the one from which I hope to retire. It's also the one that tested me the most in terms of leadership, faith, and perseverance in the face of persecution. I'll get into more specifics in a later chapter. In this one, I want to focus on how the move came about in the first place and the events that transpired immediately before it.

The former president of the Ohio Baptist General Convention is a friend of mine. He knew that Ebenezer was in search of a new pastor because the previous one had to step down for health reasons. He thought I would be a good fit. Much like I responded to the guy who told me about Brenda, I told my friend that I wasn't interested. I was content where I was. Still, he urged me to submit my resume and I did so as a formality. I truly had no interest in leaving my church in Memphis at that time. I was so lackadaisical about the process that it was Brenda who got my resume together and submitted it on my behalf. Lo and behold, I received a call to come preach a trial sermon as a pastoral candidate. If my memory serves me correctly, this was in August of 2008.

I went, accompanied by my wife. My first impression of Ebenezer was that it was way more conservative than what I was accustomed to. I don't mean conservative in terms of beliefs, rather in style. For example, they were still singing to sheet music! It was a different experience for me. I liked the church, environment, and the city, but I wasn't convinced that Ebenezer would be home. Brenda felt differently.

A few months later, I was called back to preach again. Afterward, I received another call to say that I'd been disqualified as a candidate. I was informed that the leader of the pulpit committee reported to committee members that there was something criminal about my past that couldn't be disclosed because of the Privacy Act of 1974. From what I gathered, there was an implication of child molestation. I had informed the committee about my troubles prior to accepting my call to preach, but where the molestation charges came from is beyond me. Part of me believes it was falsified because this particular individual didn't want me to get the position. There was a group of people who wanted the retiring pastor's son to take over. Thus, in order to ensure that happened, I suppose that there were creative ways in which others were being disqualified as well. Nevertheless, because some members of the committee took it upon themselves to investigate things further, it was found that there was no truth to the allegations and I was put back into the running.

I believe I fell in love with Ebenezer when I was called back a third time in January of 2009 to preach and teach for seven weeks of prayer. This was something that the previous pastor began doing at least thirty years ago. Beginning the first Sunday after New Year's, the members of the church gather together daily for seven straight weeks to pray. The title of my message that Sunday was something to the effect of "Never let your past cancel out your destiny." I used Philippians 3:13-14 as the foundation for this sermon. **"Brethren, I count not myself to have apprehended: but this one thing I do, forgetting those things which are behind, and reaching forth unto those things which are before, I press toward the mark for the prize of the high calling of God in Christ Jesus."** February would be the month when Ebenezer called me to preach there permanently. It would also be when life would drastically change for Brenda and me.

My wife wanted me to get the position at Ebenezer so badly that she prayed for it to happen daily. There were even times when she fasted. I did neither. It was one of those things where I was okay no matter how God decided to work things out. If I stayed in Memphis, amen. If I didn't, amen. Brenda's motivation for me to go there was because she felt like I'd sacrificed a lot to start over in Memphis. My church in White Sulphur Springs was growing in ministry, members, and monetarily. That wasn't necessarily the case at our current church, at least financially. For starters, the original church I began preaching at was called New Jerusalem Missionary Baptist Church. It was a small building that sat behind a cemetery. The church had gone through some difficulties and was in a lot of debt. They couldn't afford to pay a pastor at the time I started, but I took the job anyhow with the understanding that I would get paid after the church was debt-free. The Lord blessed us to turn things around within a year under my leadership.

After New Jerusalem was out of financial trouble, that's when mess started happening. There was a lot of internal conflict. All of a sudden, the trustees didn't want me to be in the room when the money was being counted. It's not that I *had* to be there. There were times I was and times when I wasn't. What bothered me is that it became an issue that sprung out of nowhere, as far as I was aware. Some members of the church took me to court over simple stuff. For example, I was sued about the location where the church van would be parked. It was crazy. Little did I know, this experience was preparing me for what was to come at Ebenezer. There was a great divide between congregants at New Jerusalem who supported me and those who didn't. One of things that they disagreed upon was expansion. Some of us wanted to purchase a daycare and use it to open a school. Others did not. Again, this was a foreshadowing of things to come.

Before I began preaching at New Jerusalem, there was a clause in the bylaws which stated that they would vote on a pastor every year. One of my conditions of accepting the position was that the clause be removed. They agreed, but after all the drama took place, they wanted to re-insert it. After the court battles, the end result was that the church split. It was something I later learned had been done four times since the founder had started it. There was so much damage done that, on New Year's Day in 2000, I preached my first sermon at Greater New Jerusalem Missionary Baptist Church in a building that Brenda and I financed ourselves.

Things were going great at the "new" church ministry wise. The congregation began to mirror that of the very first church I pastored in Williamson, West Virginia. There was nothing financial that made it significant. It was the ministry that took place. To see the recovering drug addicts, alcoholics, and HIV victims, along with those who had full-blown AIDS, that were saved and baptized was richer than any check that could have ever been written. God was sending people who were there to worship Him. One of the piano players had a life sentence for murder overturned. She also testified about how the Lord had delivered her from lesbianism. About five people in the choir were afflicted with AIDS. There were also reformed gang members and former homeless people that made up our congregation. These are the people that society views as "lower" class citizens, but they were high on the Heavenly roll call. Thus, when the opportunity to be at Ebenezer was presented, I wasn't overjoyed. God was already working through me in a mighty way. (For the record, I want to say that I now thank God for being at Ebenezer. I thank Him for my wife and my friend who were both praying for my favor when I didn't have sense enough to do so myself. In addition, I thank Him for the members who lobbied on my behalf and wouldn't accept the pulpit committee leader's word about me.)

About five days before I received word that Ebenezer had selected me to be their pastor, my wife had an accident. On February 7 in 2009, Brenda was changing the light bulb on that mid-Saturday afternoon. She was standing in a chair and somehow lost her balance. She fell, breaking her leg at the knee in three places. Home alone in excruciating pain and immobile, Brenda crawled to the phone and called our youngest daughter, Brittany, who called 9-1-1. You're probably wondering why Brenda didn't call 9-1-1 herself. That's a good question! Because I know my wife is an intelligent woman, I'm going to chalk it up to deliriousness as a result of the fall. In any event, Brittany got help. When the squad arrived, they had to knock in the door because it was locked and Brenda was unable to get to it.

The girls and I met Brenda at the hospital where doctors tied her leg on a stint and said they were going to keep her until Monday when they would put pins in it. For whatever reason, they didn't do pins on the weekends. Sunday morning, I went to check on Brenda before service and the baby girl told me that her mother wasn't looking right. Sure enough, Brenda's face was distorted and she felt very cold. I called the doctor into the room and he speculated that it was either the morphine or a stroke. Suspecting a stroke, my wife was transported via helicopter to a hospital in downtown Memphis that specialized in caring for stroke victims.

At Brenda's urging, I went to church. I was scheduled as a guest preacher at a place where Brenda was good friends with the pastor's wife. I would have canceled my appearance at the church in a heartbeat's notice, but

Brenda did not want me to. The resilience that my wife had to support me in ministry while doped up on morphine and pending confirmation about whether or not she'd had a stroke is remarkable. Personally, I don't know many women who would not have demanded that their husbands remain by their bedside. This, again, points to my being blessed with a woman who understands that to whom much is given, much is required (Luke 12:48). Though I am the preacher, when all is said and done, we are in ministry together. Without her, I could not do all that I do. Anyhow, I went to guest preach at the early service of the other pastor's church and also preached the regular service at my own. Immediately afterward, I went to the hospital where Brenda had been taken and learned that she had indeed had a stroke. The girls and I were assured by doctors that all would be fine. We were told that we could go home that night. It was around 4 a.m. Monday morning when I was called to the hospital to make a life or death decision concerning my wife.

Personal Reflections

1. Have you ever sued someone or been sued? What was the experience like for you? In the end, was "justice" served?

2. In 1 Corinthians 6:1-8, Paul speaks against Christians taking each other to court. What are some of the spiritual damages for believers and unbelievers when Christians bring lawsuits against one another?

3. Do you agree with the decision to preach that Sunday morning after Brenda was hospitalized? Why or why not?

Chapter 12: Another Blended Mess

When the doctors called me into the ICU early that Monday morning, it was because Brenda's brain had swollen. They said they needed to cut open her skull in order to alleviate the pressure to the brain. I was told that it would be a miracle if she lived five to seven days because so much damage had already been done to her brain. It was expanding fast. The doctors had no prognosis of what her condition would be after the surgery. There was the risk that she could be permanently paralyzed on the side affected by the stroke. In addition, there was a possibility that Brenda would be brain dead and a vegetable for the rest of her life.

The doctors spoke to the entire family, including the girls and Brenda's parents, but ultimately the decision was mine because Brenda was not coherent enough to decide for herself. It was, by all sense of the phrase, a catch-22. If Brenda didn't have the surgery, she could die or be comatose indefinitely. If she did have the surgery, she could die or be comatose indefinitely. When I informed the family that Brenda and I had discussed these types of situations and I knew she did not want a sub-quality of life, an all-out family war broke loose.

When Hezekiah was about to die, the Lord sent word to him through the prophet Isaiah saying, **"Set thine house in order: for thou shalt die, and not live"** (Isaiah 38:1). If you don't have your medical wishes documented, whatever they may be, please share them with your extended family in addition to your spouse. I strongly urge everyone to get your wishes in writing because, even if you communicate them, you never know how your family will act during a time of crisis. I encourage you to have both a living will and a medical power of attorney to prevent any confusion about your financial affairs or your health.

I had to tell my daughters and Brenda's parents that she did not want to be an invalid. I had to share with them that Brenda had said if ever the day came and she wouldn't be "normal," to let her go on to Heaven. They blew up. It wasn't telling the doctors not to do the surgery. I was telling the family and the doctors what Brenda wanted in the event that things didn't go right. It was rough being the mouthpiece for my wife and being attacked by her loved ones for a decision that Brenda had already made. I stood firm, but not without turmoil. Not only did I have to deal with it, but so did Kristen. When Brenda was sick, it became clear that our "blended" family was simply a circle with a line drawn down the middle. Ashley and Brittany were on one side with my in-laws; Kristen and I were on the other. Things got so ugly that my mother-in-law went off on Kristen, telling her that she wasn't part of the family and had no say in the decision-making.

Keep in mind that this was in 2009. Brenda and I had been married nearly fourteen years by that time. Brenda and Kristen had worked out their issues, but this incident made my daughter feel like she was the black sheep of the family. She felt unwanted and undervalued. That angered me. Eventually Ashley caught flak from my mother-in-law as well because she was sympathetic to my side of things. Ashley didn't necessarily agree with me regarding her mother, but she was more understanding than the rest of the family. For that, she was called two-faced by her grandmother. To say that there was a family feud would be an understatement. As I stated in the beginning of the chapter, it was a war.

Things were touch and go after the surgery. One moment Brenda would look like she would pull through; a few minutes later, all signs would point to her dying. It was a very traumatic and emotional experience that lasted a little over three weeks. In the midst of all that was going on, I received a letter from Ebenezer stating that they wanted me to be their pastor. I couldn't celebrate because of what Brenda was experiencing. The letter also troubled me. Brenda was the one who fasted and prayed for me to get the position. I was bothered by the fact that she might not live to see that God had answered her prayer. I prayed that He would preserve her life so that she could enjoy the journey as well.

Ironically, I'm not sure that I would have accepted the offer had Brenda not gotten ill. As I said previously, I was content as the pastor of Greater New Jerusalem. Brenda's sickness caused me to rethink things. If she didn't make it through, I wanted to go someplace and have a fresh start.

The blow up with my mother-in-law, in particular, really got to me. If Brenda did make it, our entire financial responsibility would be on my shoulders. Brenda made over $65,000 a year at her job. No one knew the final outcome of her condition, but one thing that was certain is that she wouldn't be the same. I pastored a church where the people didn't have much to pay. I was fine with that when our family's income was subsidized with the car lot I owned and Brenda's salary. Now that she wouldn't be able to keep her job, I needed to find a way to make up the difference so we could stay above water.

Once we got past the critical weeks of ups and downs with Brenda's condition after the surgery, she began showing signs of improvement. There was a trach tube inside her throat so she couldn't speak. She communicated to us through writing. I waited a few days before telling her that I had accepted the offer at Ebenezer. When I did, she was ecstatic. We also had the support from the deacons and trustees at our church. Only one of them said that I needed to stay; the other seven thought I should accept the offer. They weren't happy to see Brenda and me leave, but they understood that the decision was best for our family.

I preached my first sermon as the Pastor of Ebenezer on Palm Sunday in April of 2009. For those who don't know, Palm Sunday is a week before Easter and it's a celebration of Jesus's triumphant entry into Jerusalem before His crucifixion and resurrection.[5] Brenda, still recovering from her surgery, wasn't able to move with me at first, so I spent a lot of time going back and forth between Memphis, Tennessee and Sandusky, Ohio. There's about seven hundred miles between the two places. I smirk thinking about the distance because it's eerily similar to how far I had to drive when we were dating. The things we do for the people we love . . . Gas was way more expensive in 2009 than it was in 1994, but where there is the Lord, there is a way. It was tiring, but I did it because of my love for her. She was and is my bride.

It was the middle part of May when Brenda was able to join me in Sandusky. I would transport her back and forth from our home to service in a wheelchair because she was unable to walk. The doctors never got around to putting pins in her leg. The stroke had taken precedence and eventually the pins were no longer needed because she'd been confined to the bed, unable to move her leg. Every Sunday I wheeled Brenda into the sanctuary for service. It was about a year before she was able to walk in on her own after a lot of prayer, therapy, and patience.

There were additional health issues that arose and, unfortunately, Brenda had to spend more time in the hospital. During the short while we lived apart, me in Sandusky and her in Memphis, she'd hurt her hip by falling somehow in the bathroom. The doctors in Memphis didn't find anything wrong, but I kept telling them that something wasn't right. Her hip was bruised, swollen, and had a huge knot. The doctors ignored my pleas to examine her thoroughly. They said it was a side-effect of taking blood thinners. After she moved to Sandusky, I took her to see a bone specialist and we learned that she'd dislocated her hip bone. It had been out of joint for so long that the only solution was to do a hip ball replacement. This was on top of the therapy she was already receiving after breaking her leg, plus the stroke, and swelling of the brain.

This was a trying time for us. I noticed that Brenda's self-confidence had diminished because of her physical limitations. The stroke and hip surgery had affected her physical ability. She now walks with a limp and is slightly crippled on her left side. Brenda was used to being a diva (in the good sense of the word). In her mind, she'd lost some of her swagger. Quite frankly, I still think she's as beautiful as ever, inside and out. The entire ordeal gave me a new appreciation of her. She'd made a miraculous recovery and that, in and of itself, was a blessing to me. She'd unselfishly prayed for me regarding the position at Ebenezer. I was happy that she would get to reap the benefits of the prayers that she'd sown.

Initially, Brenda's side of the family was supportive of our move to Sandusky. They were under the impression that I would go first and that Brenda would recuperate in Memphis and join me possibly a year later. My wife wasn't having that. She was ready to get to Sandusky as soon as she possibly could. When, about a month or so after I moved, we informed them that she was coming as well, more family strife broke out. It was as bad, if not worse than the feud we had regarding the surgery. Ultimately, Brenda and I were a united front and withstood any backlash from family members. It also helped that the congregants of Ebenezer were good to us when we arrived. Though it would get rough in the months to come,

I am forever grateful for the outpouring of love and support that the members showed us during this time. I didn't know it then, but a storm was brewing and I was headed straight into its eye.

Personal Reflections

1. Do you know the wishes of your loved ones should a medical crisis occur?

2. Have you shared the steps that you want your family to take if you were in a life or death situation? Do you have your desires documented?

3. Have you ever been the caregiver for a loved one? Reflect on some of the blessings and stresses of being in the caregiving position.

Chapter 13: The End of Our Honeymoon

Some people believe that lightening doesn't strike in the same place twice. Whether or not that is true in the meteorological world, I can't say. I can tell you with assurance that it's not true in the spiritual world. Sometimes we get hit with the same problems that we thought we'd gotten past in years prior. There are a variety of reasons why we may experience trials, some repeatedly. It could be because we have sinned. It could be due to the fact that we didn't get the lesson the first time. Or, it could be simply for God to show Himself mighty and strong in the situation. I'm reminded of the story that John tells in chapter 9, versus 1-3, **"And as Jesus passed by, he saw a man which was blind from his birth. And his disciples asked him, saying, 'Master, who did sin, this man, or his parents, that he was born blind?' Jesus answered, 'Neither hath this man sinned, nor his parents: but that the works of God should be made manifest in him.'"**

We may also go through troubles in order to help someone else. There are times in which the way we handle our suffering ministers to others. The bottom line is that God is sovereign and we must trust Him, even when we don't understand why certain things take place (Proverbs 3:5-6). He, alone, knows the reasons behind our trials. I can speculate all I want, but in the end, the only thing I know for sure is that there has never been anything that has taken place in my life (or yours) that God has not first approved. If He let us in on all the details, we would never step forward in faith. Had He informed me of the spiritual migraines I would endure at Ebenezer when a group of members tried to have me ousted, I would have never said yes to the assignment. Consequently, I would have missed a great opportunity to see the words of Romans 8:28 come true, **"And we know that all things work together for good to them that love God, to them who are the called according to his purpose."**

By April 2012, my wife was back and forth between Sandusky and Memphis once again. Because of her medical insurance, she is required to see doctors in the state of Tennessee. When we first moved to Sandusky, she was on COBRA and could see doctors anywhere. After a year, COBRA ended and she was approved for Social Security disability. I don't know all the logistics of how the insurance plan works, but I do know that, since then, she's been limited to seeing doctors in Tennessee for any long-term care needs.

April 2012 was also when I was celebrating my third pastoral anniversary at Ebenezer. By that time, the church had some loud dissenters in our midst. Uncannily similar to what happened with New Jerusalem in Memphis, the issue was over an expansion. Back in October of 2011, Ebenezer voted to add an educational wing and some members were against it. It happened to be some of the same members who never wanted me as the pastor in the first place. Consequently, a smear campaign against me began after the church went forth with the building project.

In a way, I was prepared. The experience at New Jerusalem taught me to internalize the words of 1 Corinthians 15:58, **"Therefore, my beloved brethren, be ye stedfast, unmoveable, always abounding in the work of the Lord, forasmuch as ye know that your labour is not in vain in the Lord."** Had I truly had mal-intentions as I was accused at New Jerusalem and at Ebenezer, I would not have survived, especially at Ebenezer. It got so bad that the church held a special meeting and the congregation voted to excommunicate several members who were key players in causing the disturbance. I know that sounds harsh to some of you, but this was all done after several attempts by me and other leaders to speak with the members about their divisive behavior. They'd tricked people into signing petitions by telling them it was to call a church meeting, when in reality, the petition was to try and get me voted out. When people discovered this duplicity, they were upset and asked to have their names taken off the list.

Another thing some of the naysayers did was call the banks, bad-mouthing me trying to stop the loan for our building project from going through. They contacted architects, telling them not to proceed with the project. It was an all-out attack on my character that made front page in the news. They were attacking me, but they were making Ebenezer and the entire Body of Christ look bad with their tactics. Something had to be done.

The End of Our Honeymoon

On March 8, 2012, we held a meeting to bring the accusers before the church. There were four individuals who were the main culprits in sowing discord. Each of them had a chance to say their piece before the members of the church took a vote to decide whether or not they should remain part of our congregation. Only one person humbled himself and apologized. The other three arrogantly refused to admit to any wrongdoing, claiming that their actions had been justified. In the end, those three were voted out of the church while the first man was not.

In the meeting, the members of the church made it clear that excommunication wasn't indefinite. Rather, we left the door open for the possibility of reconciliation at a later time. Both excommunication and reconciliation are in line with Paul's teachings in 1 Corinthians 5:1-8 and 2 Corinthians 2:3-11. We, the leaders of the church and the congregation, tried to do what was right in a loving and biblical way (Matthew 18:15-17).

Unfortunately, those who lost their membership privileges decided to ignore the decision of the church and, the following Sunday, they showed up to service as if the meeting had never taken place. That wouldn't have necessarily been a problem if they would have come peacefully. However, they were disruptive during service and some church leaders called the police to have them escorted out. Sadly, being excommunicated from the church and later removed from the building didn't stop these people. The next month, when the members of Ebenezer were celebrating my third anniversary, a tent was put up in front of the church by this group, including the man who had apologized, asking people to vote me out.

Keep in mind that they had no legal authority to have this "meeting." By this time, they were no longer members of the church. Furthermore, most of the folks that they were getting to side with them were not part of Ebenezer either. They were passersby who, from the extremely skewed media reports, formed an opinion and sided with my accusers to have me removed as the pastor. I was called the anti-Christ, a criminal, a pimp, and everything else one could think of that was contrary to being a child of God. An example of some of the things that were circulated can be found on the next pages. (Note: With the exception of redacting the address on the letter sent to my wife, none of the documents have been edited. They were all scanned as received and re-sized to fit on the pages of this book.)

Dear City Officials,

We are asking that you support our right to conduct a meeting to vote on the church grounds, for the sole purpose of the removal of Clayton Eugene Howard, as the pastor of Ebenezer Baptist Church on Friday, April 27, 2012 at 6:00 P.M.

Thank you for your support,

Ebenezer Baptist Church Members

The End of Our Honeymoon

SAD 3rd YEAR ANNIVERSARY

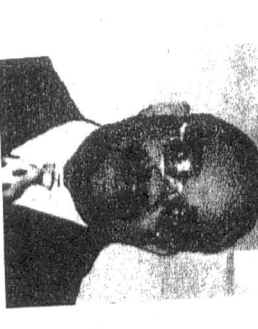

Michael Clyde Tanyhill

(AKA) Also Known As

A Criminal THEN...' A Criminal NOW

IN YOUR SEARCH FOR STATUS AND PRESTIGE, YOU WERE NOT PREPARED FOR THE ORDEALS AND SACRIFICES INVOLVED IN TRUE LEADERSHIP. IT'S BEEN 3 LONG ARDUOUS YEARS, FULL OF TURMOIL, SINCE YOUR COMING TO THIS CITY. YOU LIED TO THE MEMBERS OF EBENEZER BAPTIST CHURCH, TO GET THE POSITION AS PASTOR, *FLUNKED* CHRISTIAN EDUCATION COURSES, PUT THE CHURCH IN A *MILLION* DOLLAR DEBT, HAVE *SCATTERED* THE FLOCK LIKE NO OTHER, *LIED* TO THE MEMBERS ABOUT THE FINANCES, HAD ATTEMPTED VERBAL AND PHYSICAL *BRAWLS* WITH MINISTERS, AND YOU CAUSED THE MEMBERSHIP TO BE SUPREMELY *FOCUSED* ON, AND GIVE UNDIVIDED *ATTENTION* TO, THE CONSTANT *CALAMITY* AND ONGOING *PROBLEMS*, THAT YOU HAVE CAUSED THIS CHURCH. WE THE MEMBERS ASK IS THIS THE *FULFILLING* OF THE GREAT COMMISSION?

NO!

THESE ARE CRIMES AGAINST THE BODY OF CHRIST.

THIS BODY OF BELIEVERS HAS THE RIGHT TO KNOW, THAT YOU ARE A CONVICTED **FELON**, WHO PLEADED GUILTY TO THE OFFENSE OF BURGLARY.

YOU STOLE MONEY AND HAD TO PAY IT BACK. CLAYTON, YOU WERE SENTENCED TO THE OHIO STATE REFORMATORY FOR A MINIMUM OF 2 YEARS, AND A MAXIMUM OF 15 YEARS FOR BURGLARY. YOU WERE ON PROBATION FOR 5 YEARS IN CHARGE OF A N. WOODRUFF, WHO WAS PLACED OVER YOU, AS YOUR PROBATION OFFICER.

THAT'S NOT THE **PROBLEM**, WHICH WE FACE HERE IN THIS CITY, WITH YOU THOUGH.

THE PROBLEM **IS**, THAT YOU HAVE **NOT CHANGED.**

Sister Brenda Gardner Howard

Memphis, TN. 38141-0248

April 18, 2012

Dear Sister Brenda Haith-Howard,

There are not enough words to describe how precious Pastors are, but unfortunately your husband does not fit into that category. It seems you were in on it all the time. You were in "co-hoots" with your crooked spouse to rob and destroy our fine church. As we look upon you with pity, we wonder just what were you thinking about this so called man of God you have dropped off on us. We want you to TAKE him back with you and keep him down there with you.

Please know this one thing however; that we know you are an abused women and is still greatly in need of prayer, but your need does not give you the right to take our kindness for a weakness, to benefit your pimp wannabe preacher husband.

We will rid ourselves of him and hope not to see you anymore. As we worship with your husband and look at this crook perform every Sunday, know this one thang.....We hate him for what he stands for and for what he has and is doing to our church. The extensive background investigation has uncovered and exposed all of his illusive, deceptive, carnal, and apostate carrying on. How dare he come to Ebenezer with all of this witchery baggage to destroy, scatter and separate? Did you and "Tanyhill" think you had struck pay dirt once your eyes feasted on our finances? Yes, we do know about Tanyhill and all of his crimes. Yes, we do know about the destruction of his last 3 churches and the robbery of God that went along with his schemes.

The theme for your anniversary "Fulfillment of the Great Commission" could not have come at a better time, or maybe at a very inopportune time. Look at God and how the fulfillment of the GREAT COMMISSION is working. You have confessed to know the bible and God's word, so direct your attention to Mark chapter 13 and St. John chapter 14 and 17. These messages are from God. Watch for the things that are coming! Stand on HIS word! And lastly, this battle is the LORD'S!!

May God Himself, reward him for his deeds.

Prayerfully,

Your support at Ebenezer

Your support at Ebenezer

Note: Due to the fact that the letter on this page may be illegible in its original state, it has been re-typed verbatim and included in Appendix C on page 115.

The End of Our Honeymoon

These dissenting members were relentless in their attempts to have things go their way. Had a few of the leaders and I not lingered at the church after the anniversary celebration, we would have been locked out. The group who organized the tent "meeting" had called a locksmith who, without any proper documentation or authority, was going to change the locks of the church. One of the deacons went to Walmart to buy chains to put on the insides of the doors to keep the locksmith from coming in.

Does all of this sound crazy? It should! I couldn't make this stuff up if I tried. I was undeniably hurt by everything that was happening. They were ruthless. What especially made me angry was the letter on the previous page that was sent to my wife. (See also Appendix C on page 115.)

Everyone was well aware of Brenda's health problems. She was at her parents' house during this time recovering from surgery and also still mourning the recent loss of her mother. The congregation knew about all of this and yet, someone ignorantly sent Brenda these hateful words all supposedly in the Name of Jesus. I wondered how anyone could do such a thing. Then again, there were rumors going around that Brenda wasn't really crippled.

Some people said that Brenda's medical conditions were all a front in my/our efforts to dupe the church. These were some of the same people who visited her months earlier on her 49th birthday when she was in a rehab center in Lorain, Ohio, a town located about thirty minutes east of Sandusky. Did they think we got the rehabilitation facility to go along with our so-called façade as well? Absurd!

I'm a big boy, spiritually-speaking. Physically, I'm a little over five feet, six and a half inches. The point is, I can handle people messing with me more than I can with them messing with my wife. Messing with me was one thing, but dragging my wife into the middle of nonsense, especially considering her condition, made me want to resurrect "Fast Chili" in the sense of taking this fight to the streets. Thankfully, my flesh lost this battle and the spirit of God within me took over. I didn't curse or hit anyone, though there were times I wanted to. With the help of the Lord, I humbled myself and prayed for everyone.

Personal Reflections

1. Read Romans 8:28. If you truly believe the words of this Scripture, reflect on a time when it has proven to be true in your own life.

2. Do you think the decision to excommunicate members from Ebenezer was too harsh? Why or why not? What would you have done differently?

3. There are times when life's circumstances can tempt the old ways of our flesh to rise up. Read 2 Corinthians 5:17. How does being a "new creation" in Christ help you to overcome the flesh with His spirit?

Chapter 14: Growing Pains

I know some people are going to say that I came to Ebenezer with my own agenda to build because the project at New Jerusalem didn't happen. That couldn't be further from the truth. Did I have a vision to build at New Jerusalem? Yes. Did I have a vision to build at Ebenezer? Yes. One didn't influence the other. If anything, they were both birthed from my desire to educate God's people.

I learned from others that the previous pastor had tried to expand Ebenezer in years prior. For whatever reason, he was not successful. His desire to renovate stemmed from the building's space limitations. As it originally stood, there was no room for Sunday school classes. They used partitions in the fellowship hall to create makeshift classrooms. I added to his idea in that I wanted an educational wing. I was looking beyond simply having space for Sunday school. My dream was to have room for an after-school program and other things. Thus, it's fair to say that what I had in mind was a little more extravagant than the former pastor's idea. When our visions were combined, the end result was an added section comprised of a computer lab, office space, library, exercise room, and eight classrooms. (I want to note that I did not speak with the previous pastor directly. All of this was communicated to me from others who worked with him. By the time I came on board to Ebenezer, he had been afflicted with Alzheimer's.)

Some of the plans for enhancing the fellowship hall had been drawn prior to my arrival at Ebenezer. Some leaders had shared them with me and began talking to me about this before I officially assumed my role as the new pastor. I accepted the job expecting to break ground eventually. My initial time at Ebenezer was spent getting to know the congregants and vice versa. I also took time to walk around and pray over the grounds for God's will to be done. Though I knew what had been discussed regarding renovations, I didn't want to move outside of His timing.

It was around November of 2009 when, during our annual meeting, the church voted unanimously to go forward with investigating the building project. We didn't vote to build. Our vote was to research the costs and gather all necessary information we needed in order to later decide on expansion. The committee spent nearly all of 2010 searching and collecting information. It wasn't until approximately June of 2011 when we started to break ground. By that time, those who weren't in agreement had begun to rear their heads.

One of their criticisms of me is that I didn't bring information to the congregants on a regular basis. I will give them that accusation. It is true. What is not true is that I was purposely trying to be secretive or deceive anyone. The reason why I didn't bombard the congregation with details consistently was because I didn't have anything to share. I didn't think it would be wise to give them bits and pieces of information that was inconclusive. Confusion happens that way. My philosophy was to only come before the congregation when there were hardcore facts about the bids, financial rates, and other information pertinent to the expansion project. When we, the committee, had details, members of the usher board, missionary society, deaconate board, and the official church board came together to discuss all of the options and there was another vote. There was an overwhelming number of members who wanted to proceed with the building project, a handful of no's, and a few who abstained. It was those who were against us moving forward who took what was said in the meetings, twisted the words, and started discord within the congregation.

Change, even positive ones, can be difficult for people who are complacent. It is my personal belief that the dissenters were such. In their defense, a disruption to their norm made them uncomfortable. In addition, the church was debt-free so the concept of getting a loan frightened them. I understood that concern. That's why the committee and I worked diligently to get the best possible deals all across the board. What I didn't understand then and I still don't now, is why they allowed their objections to reach such horrendous levels of disrespect and hatred. No, I wasn't going to have meetings every time someone asked or to address all the accusations against me. I was determined not to entertain foolishness. Yet, foolishness found a way to entertain itself at the most inopportune times.

An example of foolery happened one Sunday morning around October of 2011 when one of the deacons stood up in the middle of service to demand a church meeting. He had some people working with him in the sound room. They cut off my mic so I couldn't speak, but every word he said was heard. That, in and of itself, was wrong, but imagine the impression it left with people who were visiting our church that morning because it was Friends and Family Day. The way this deacon operated was disrespectful all across the board. In the end, neither I, nor the other deacons or trustees would authorize the meeting. It was out of order. Plus, the sole purpose was to try and stop us from going forth with the expansion project. It was too late by that time. The majority had already voted.

For the record, the "majority rules" principle is not to imply that the majority is always right. In the Gospels, it was the majority who wanted to crucify Jesus (Luke 23:20-21). In our society, it's the majority who seek to overturn the godly order of things. I make these statements because I don't want it to seem like I went with the crowd simply for the sake of doing so. If the majority had voted in favor of the project and I felt in my spirit that we were out of line with God's will, I would have strongly voiced my objections. I went with the crowd because their actions confirmed the vision that had already been placed in my spirit. The crowd plus Jesus will be right every time. The Lord had given me a vision of the church and, as the pastor, it was my responsibility to see that it was carried out. Proverbs 29:18 states, **"Where there is no vision, the people perish: but he that keepeth the law, happy is he."**

Anyone who has a vision will also have people who try to deter you from accomplishing it. In the book of Nehemiah, we learn that the prophet faced opposition when it came to rebuilding the walls of Jerusalem. Chapter 4 of Nehemiah is a perfect example of the cycle of advancements and setbacks when it comes to accomplishing a goal. If God has instructed you to do something, it does not mean you will breeze to the finish line without a few hurdles along the way. As the saying goes, "faith makes everything possible, not easy." God will take care of your enemies, but He won't necessarily remove them. Nehemiah and his builders had to proceed despite criticism received from their opponents.

Opposition doesn't mean that one is doing something wrong. Again, the prophet Nehemiah was doing the right thing, yet he and those helping him incited anger from people around them (Nehemiah 4:1-7). They were mocked (Nehemiah 4:2) and threatened (Nehemiah 4:8, 11-12). The people responded to these things by praying (Nehemiah 4:4-5, 9) and they continued the work that was set in their hearts (Nehemiah 4:6). In essence, that's what we did at Ebenezer. We continued to work, despite being opposed.

The opposing voices started small and then grew loud to the point where the local media got involved. Reporters from the *Sandusky Register* jumped on the bandwagon of the naysayers and printed negative things about me. The reporters also dug up the "dirt" about my experiences at New Jerusalem in Memphis and ran with it. Every story that appeared in the paper was as if what was being said about me was true. The dissenting members of Ebenezer hired a private investigator to find things out about my past. I'd already disclosed my criminal history before I was hired, yet, they found it necessary to pay for a detective. Some good he did. The church lawyers obtained a report of his "findings." In it, it's mentioned that I once shared an address with a Rosa Howard and that this person could possibly be an ex-wife. Um . . . *wrong!* They could have saved their money and come to me. I would have told them that she was my mother! Her name, by the way, was Rosa Lee Howard.

I found it so disgraceful that a private church disagreement had been dragged into the public. The opponents took me to court to remove me as pastor. This was *after* they had been voted out the church. Excommunication was our last resort in efforts to remove the cancerous members from among us. It was the only way we knew how to stop the nonsense. The truth of the matter is that they all decided their own fate. They'd been given a choice: to stop the chaos or be expelled from the church. They chose to continue the drama and we took action to make it cease. It didn't work because they continued with the letters and the attempted tent ousting, mentioned in the last chapter. Some of them went as far as to ride around with a bumper sticker expressing their disdain for me. It read, "Restore Ebenezer; Remove Howard."

The church attorney sent a threatening letter in hopes of putting a halt to their actions. It was futile. Nothing was going to sway them. I was hurt by the attacks on my character. I was more grieved about what their actions did to hurt the Body of Christ. What hope do unsaved people have when people who claim to know Jesus act foolish? As I'm sure you can imagine, people were quick to fill the web with comments about why they didn't go to church or trust pastors. After the mess they were reading in the papers, who could blame them? As Christians, we have a responsibility to let the light of Jesus shine through us. It is through our light that we can draw others to glorify Him (Matthew 5:16). When we exemplify ugliness and contempt, we bring shame to Jesus's name.

Personal Reflections

1. Why do you think God allows us to experience opposition when trying to accomplish divinely-inspired goals?

2. Why does change, even positive ones, make people feel uncomfortable?

3. Imagine you were in the sanctuary during the Friends and Family Day service when the disruption with the deacon took place. What would your overall opinion of Ebenezer have been? Would that experience have influenced how you felt about church in general?

Chapter 15: Truth, Lies, & Consequences

There's a saying that a lie will make it halfway across the world before the truth puts its pants on. Thanks to the reporters, the lies about me circulated swiftly. It hurt, but not to the point that I was deterred from my vision. In a way, I believe the experience in Memphis at New Jerusalem had prepared me. I like to say that fire can't burn where fire has already been. I'd dealt with contrary members before, so that, in and of itself, wasn't new to me. The level of the attacks were like nothing I'd ever experienced previously. Even still, God granted me peace that passed even my own understanding (Philippians 4:7). I didn't spend a single night tossing or turning over anything that was happening. What gave me peace, then and now, is the fact that I know, in my heart, I didn't intentionally do anything wrong or attempt to mislead anyone in any manner. My conscience was clear and my God was in control.

The stuff that went down caught me off guard, but it didn't catch God by surprise. He knew from the moment I accepted the assignment to preach at Ebenezer that a storm was in the near future. It didn't feel good going through it. However, I consider it a spiritual honor that God trusted me with such persecution. James 1:2 says to **"count it all joy"** when trouble comes our way. This doesn't mean that we'll go around skipping and singing, "Zip-a-Dee-Doo-Dah" each time we are hit with a blindside. What we can do is keep in mind that nothing we experience on earth will come close to the suffering that Jesus endured on our behalf. God can't trust everyone to handle trouble well. The question is, can He trust *you*?

Billionaire Warren Buffet has been quoted as saying that it takes twenty years to build a reputation and five minutes to ruin it.[6] There is a lot of truth in that statement. As a child, I'd built a reputation for being mischievous. As a teen, I was rebellious. Throughout my teenage years until well into my twenties, I was known as a drug dealer and as a lover of ladies. These, and other labels, were all well-deserved. I have never been an angel.

Some of the things that were said about me by my opponents were downright absurd. For example, the letter on page 74 (see also Appendix C) that was written to my wife states that she was an abused woman. It's crazy how, when people don't have legitimate allegations to throw at you, they make them up. I have never been abusive to my wife or any woman, for that matter. Even in all my shady dealings with women in my street days, I didn't get down like that. As a matter of fact, I have very little respect for any man who puts his hands abusively on a woman. Personally, I believe that the average man who would beat a woman wouldn't hit a man. When one of my ex-girlfriends tried pouring hot, scalding grease on me, I didn't retaliate with my fists. "Fast Chili" got fast feet and got out of the way and far from her for good. I don't care how much mouth or attitude a female has, no man has a right to lay a finger on her in a negative way. That's cowardly behavior and something that makes me sick to my stomach. I have never laid a hand on my wife in such manner. It's not like I pushed Brenda off the chair to cause her injuries; she fell.

I was also accused of not attending college. I did attend, but I never graduated from any place. I mentioned in Chapter 5 how insecure I was about not being formally educated. My motivation for marrying my first wife, Diana, was because she was smart and I thought she would help me in terms of teaching me some skills I would need to successfully complete a college program. That never happened. Instead of a traditional student, I consider myself a student of the Word in God's divine classroom.

God taught me that man doesn't need to qualify me for something He's already certified me to do. I am still very much pro-education. I hate reading, but I do it because it's a way to acquire knowledge. Due to my longevity and work in ministry, I've been awarded honorary degrees over the years. Yes, the degrees were listed on my resume as well as the years I attended certain colleges. The purpose of a resume is to make a candidate look good for whatever position he/she is applying. Details are given about specifics when asked. Call it residual insecurity about not being formally educated and wanting to dress up my resume, but don't call it a lie. I do have the degrees. When being considered for the pastoral position at Ebenezer, the committee left no stone unturned. Any questions about my educational training was made abundantly clear during the interview process.

Some of the criminal accusations against me were true, but not revealed in their proper context. I did a lot more than what the "private investigator" reported to those who tried to get me removed. My crimes were before I accepted Jesus as my personal Lord and Savior. I have been forgiven and I know it. Thus, I would not allow man to convict me of things that the Lord had already freed me from. I refuse to be a prisoner of my past. You don't have to be either. If you have not yet accepted Jesus into your life, once again, I would like to direct your attention to Appendix A found on page 93. He can and will free you from the bondage of your sins.

If you have accepted Jesus and you are still walking around in shame, the truth of the matter is that you have not accessed all the power that has been granted to you by His Holy Spirit. No matter what it is that you have done, don't allow yourself or others to beat you up about things that are covered by Jesus's death on the cross. He didn't die for you or me to live in shame about our mistakes. He died to forgive us of all of our transgressions and to set us free from sin's grip on our eternity. Always remember that, **"If the Son therefore shall make you free, ye shall be free indeed"** (John 8:36).

Personal Reflections

1. Our attitude about problems has a direct impact on the peace (or lack thereof) we experience in the midst of our trials. Think of two separate difficult situations in your life — one when you handled things with a good attitude and another when you did not. Can you recall a difference in your stress level and overall peace in those two circumstances?

2. In general, do you think God can trust you with trouble? Explain your answer.

3. Do you think including honorary degrees on a resume is wrong? Why or why not?

Conclusion: Lessons from the Fires of Life

In general, the Book of Psalms is one of the books that I find myself reading when I need encouragement. One of my absolute favorite passages of Scripture is Psalm 139.

Each line of this passage of Scripture has so much power to me personally. It sums up my entire life, pre- and post-Christ. For example, verses 7 and 8 say, **"Whither shall I go from thy spirit? or whither shall I flee from thy presence? If I ascend up into heaven, thou art there: if I make my bed in hell, behold, thou art there."** When I read these verses, I think about all the years that I spent running from God. No matter where I turned, He was everywhere. I couldn't get away from Him when I tried.

When I read verses 13-16, I'm reminded that the calling on my life pre-dated the time I spent in my mother's womb. **"For thou hast possessed my reins: thou hast covered me in my mother's womb. I will praise thee; for I am fearfully and wonderfully made: marvellous are thy works; and that my soul knoweth right well. My substance was not hid from thee, when I was made in secret, and curiously wrought in the lowest parts of the earth. Thine eyes did see my substance, yet being unperfect; and in thy book all my members were written, which in continuance were fashioned, when as yet there was none of them."** The truth of the matter is that my steps were ordered by God before I was born.

Psalm 139 is comprised of twenty-four verses in all. It's the final two that summarize the words of my sincerest prayer. **"Search me, O God, and know my heart: try me, and know my thoughts: And see if there be any wicked way in me, and lead me in the way everlasting."** I want God to continually search my heart and to lead me in His way. It is His design for my life that I desire. Nothing more. Nothing less. One of the major things I've learned throughout any trial that I've encountered is to trust Him.

Trusting God is a crucial element in every situation we face. If we don't trust Him, then it's hard to cling to the Word He's given us through His Scriptures. You have to believe Him in order to believe His Word. When all the lies were being rapidly spread about me, it hurt. I could have packed up and went back to Memphis. I still have my car lot there and I'm sure, if I couldn't find another preaching job, I could have gone back to being a mechanic. In the last chapter, I repeated the quote about a lie making it halfway across the world before the truth puts on its pants. That may *seem* like it's true, but ultimately the truth is found in Proverbs 12:19, **"The lip of truth shall be established for ever: but a lying tongue is but for a moment."**

Though it hurts, we can't be discouraged by what people say about us. We must do our best to live our lives in the most righteous way possible. I admit, I failed to live up to all the standards of God after Diana and I split in terms of abstaining from sexual immorality. Could some of the trouble I endured be consequences of my rebellion? Perhaps. It is equally possible that none of the things I went through was a punishment of any kind, but rather opportunities for God to show Himself mighty and strong in the midst of opposition. That's personally how I see things. One of the greatest things I could do during all of the drama was to hold my peace and let the Lord fight my battles. Our enemies serve a purpose. They help to build our character and test our faith. David said, **"Thou preparest a table before me in the presence of mine enemies . . ."** (Psalm 23:5). Hang in there long enough and even your enemies will begin to see the blessings of the Lord in your life.

An example of the lip of truth is what God is doing now through the works at Ebenezer. Despite all of the opposition, the building project was completed and it is a success. We opened the doors for the after-school program in 2013 and it's going well. The first year I think we started with about fifteen kids. We doubled that the very next year. We are serving the needs of students and parents in our community through this ministry. Children who have been recommended by their elementary schools because they are struggling with certain subjects come to us for assistance. Parents do not pay for this service. Cedar Point, known as the roller coaster capital of the world,[7] has helped us to absorb some of the costs.

We also have qualified tutors in the form of current or retired teachers and administrators who volunteer their time. We have other volunteers who drive the church van to pick up kids with transportation issues. Every child who comes through our doors for this program receives a meal, help with their studies, and then they are able to partake in some recreational activities. What touches my heart more than anything is that a couple of children have accepted Christ and have been baptized as a direct result of their involvement with this ministry. To me, there's no greater service we can do than impact their spiritual lives in addition to their natural ones. We hope to be able to accommodate more students in the future. Furthermore, we plan to eventually expand our services to include a literacy programs for adults. We want to assist men and women in getting their GED as well as address other needs in our community. The ultimate vision is to help meet needs of those from the cradle to the grave.

I know that when I mentioned excommunicating some members in Chapter 13 it seemed extreme. I want the world to know that Ebenezer is a loving and merciful congregation. I don't believe for a second that members took pleasure in voting anyone out from the church. There was one person who apologized and the vote was for him to remain part of our congregation. Unfortunately, he turned on us again. All of the mess started with a core group of people who managed to conjure up a small following of others who left Ebenezer on their own accord. Now that the dust has settled, some of those individuals have returned. Several of them have apologized, admitting that they'd gotten caught up in the hype.

Whether you're a person who has done wrong or has been wronged, forgiveness is a necessary component of your relationship with God and others. Never be so big that you can't apologize or accept an apology. We are blessed when we are peacemakers (Mathews 5:9). I tried to appease those angry with me before by apologizing. My efforts were in vain. They wanted me to stop moving forward with an assignment I know I was to accomplish. I would not adhere to those demands. When it comes to choosing between upsetting God or people, I will choose to anger people over God every time. To anyone reading this who still has a grudge against me because of how things played out, I am truly sorry for anything that I've done to offend you. It was never my intent for Ebenezer to become fractured. I hope one day your heart will heal.

In addition to forgiveness, another lesson life has taught me is that faith and fear can't reside in the same heart in equal amounts. One will inevitably take over the other. If we live by faith, which we are called to do (Hebrews 10:38), we will be faced with times of uncertainty. I've said it several times throughout this book and I'll say it again, God doesn't give us all of the details to our assignments. We are sometimes scared to move forward because we don't have all of the information, but if He disclosed everything, we still wouldn't move. Fear is an immobilizer. Its purpose is to keep you stagnant. I would have never come to Ebenezer if I'd known all that I would have to endure to get to this point. My flesh is too weak. In the middle of the battle, my faith reminded me that it wasn't really about me. God has great plans for Ebenezer. I was the target. The one the enemy had to come after.

Anyone who leads any type of Christ-centered organization can be certain that the enemy is gunning for you. When it comes to the church, scandals involving pastors are not new. If the enemy destroys the leader's character, he will destroy the following by causing people to leave THE church. This causes people to look suspiciously at churches, in general, and say things like, "I don't trust pastors" or "all preachers are crooks." Unfortunately, there are some people who have had some real-life negative experiences with crooked pastors. The grand scheme of the enemy's plan is to get people to turn away from Jesus. He does this through real and false accusations of church leaders.

If you are someone in leadership dealing with contrary members and you know in your heart of hearts that you have not done anything wrong to them, you still have to love them. Do not render evil for evil (Romans 12:17; 1 Peter 3:9). Proverbs 10:12 states that, **"Hatred stirreth up strifes: but love covereth all sins."** 1 Peter 4:8 says it this way, **"And above all things have fervent charity among yourselves: for charity shall cover the multitude of sins."** Many people are being ignorantly used by the devil, meaning that they are unaware or simply don't care that they are doing his bidding. Whether you're a leader or not, the love of Christ has to be portrayed through you even in the midst of adversity. We can't fix people. That's God's job. You may not *like* them, but you are obligated to *love* them. God does. Showing love to people who have mistreated you is not an easy thing to do. In fact, I'd dare say that it's impossible to do on our own. If you continuously submit yourself to the Lord and earnestly seek His ways, He will love through you. Your enemies can only do so much. There is an expiration date stamped on your troubles. In the words of an old gospel song, "Run on [and] see what the end's gonna be"[8] (apostrophe added).

I thank the Lord for the members of Ebenezer who stood by me through all the negativity. They were then and still are a blessing. I love my congregation and I hope to be there with them until the day I retire to go home and be with the Lord. Ebenezer is a great church. It's not without issues, of course. We made it through a difficult storm together. I'm sure there will be others to come. Prayerfully, the worst is behind us. The circumstances didn't only strengthen me individually, but also the church. Since all has passed, we have more active members of Ebenezer now than we did when I first arrived. That's only because of God's grace. Ebenezer's reputation took a hit in the media, but God is establishing the lip of truth even as the words on this page are being read. It is to Him that all glory belongs.

Brenda and I are still facing some challenges with her health. In 2014, she almost died as a result of a blood infection. We continue to commute back and forth between Sandusky, Ohio and Memphis, Tennessee. Sometimes Brenda has to stay in Memphis for extended periods of times due to her healthcare needs. It's not easy, but we are doing what we have to do. My wife remains fully supportive of me pastoring at Ebenezer. She is a woman like none other I have ever met. I feel like God gave me the cream of the crop when Brenda came into my life. Without Brenda's love and prayers, I don't know what I would do. She loves Ebenezer as much, if not more, than I do. She and I are thankful to be on this journey together.

Though I'm not happy about some of the choices I've made in life, I can't say that I regret anything. Everything has worked together to mold and shape me into the person that I am today. Life has a tendency to make us bitter or better. Praise God that I am the latter and not the former. It's because I allowed Him to work in me. Left on my own accord, I could very well be bitter. I could point out the unfairness of all my situations and complain that God was/is not really there for me. I could walk around with a chip on my shoulder toward everyone who has talked negatively about me, lied on me, or hurt me. In the end, those actions would not do any good.

I love the story of the three Hebrew boys in Daniel 3. When faced with being thrown in the fire, they had an unwavering trust in God. It was to the point that they knew He had the power to deliver them from the fire. At the same time, they were content to burn if He chose not to do so. They recognized God's sovereignty in the situation. We need to do that in our lives as well. It is possible to go through a spiritual fire and not be singed when Jesus is with you.

It doesn't mean that you won't feel the heat of the flames. What it does mean is that you don't have to be affected by the heat and you can be better because of it. As I said two paragraphs above, life can make you bitter or better. Ultimately, the choice is yours.

Personal Reflections

1. How, if at all, does Psalm 139 minister to you?

2. Have you ever had a negative experience with someone in the church? If so, have you allowed it to impact your relationship with God?

3. "Life can make you bitter or better." Which has it done for you?

Appendix A: Prayer of Salvation

Romans 10:9-10 says, **"That if thou shalt confess with thy mouth the Lord Jesus, and shalt believe in thine heart that God hath raised him from the dead, thou shalt be saved. For with the heart man believeth unto righteousness; and with the mouth confession is made unto salvation."** Based on this Scripture, a prayer of salvation has been written out for you below.

"Dear God,

I acknowledge before You that I am a sinner. I come to You in the name of Jesus and ask that You forgive me of all of my transgressions. I believe with my whole heart that Jesus was sinless and that He took my place on the cross when He died for my sins. I believe that He was raised from the dead and is the only Lord and Savior of the world. I ask Jesus to come into my heart and cleanse me from all unrighteousness. I desire to live a life that is pleasing to You, Lord. By faith, I believe that I am saved. I believe that my past is forgiven. I believe that I have been given a clean slate. You have thrown my sins in the sea of forgetfulness and I am no longer in bondage to sin. Thank You for making me a new creature in Christ Jesus. Amen."

Congratulations! The Bible says that the angels in Heaven rejoice when a person is saved (Luke 15:10). Please surround yourself with other Bible-believing Christians as soon as you can. They will help encourage you and strengthen your walk with the Lord. If you would like me to pray for you, feel free to contact me at Ebenezer Baptist Church, 1215 Pierce Avenue, Sandusky, OH 44870.

Appendix B: Scriptures Used or Referenced

For your convenience, all Scriptures used or referenced throughout this book are listed in the order in which they first appear or are mentioned. It is strongly recommended that, whenever possible, you read from an actual Bible to get the full contextual meaning of all passages.

Foreword

1 Corinthians 12:21-25 (NKJV)
[21] And the eye cannot say to the hand, "I have no need of you"; nor again the head to the feet, "I have no need of you." [22] No, much rather, those members of the body which seem to be weaker are necessary. [23] And those members of the body which we think to be less honorable, on these we bestow greater honor; and our unpresentable parts have greater modesty, [24] but our presentable parts have no need. But God composed the body, having given greater honor to that part which lacks it, [25] that there should be no schism in the body, but that the members should have the same care for one another. (Page ix)

1 Peter 4:11
If any man speak, let him speak as the oracles of God; if any man minister, let him do it as of the ability which God giveth: that God in all things may be glorified through Jesus Christ, to whom be praise and dominion for ever and ever. Amen. (Page ix)

Introduction

Daniel 3
[1] Nebuchadnezzar the king made an image of gold, whose height was threescore cubits, and the breadth thereof six cubits: he set it up in the plain of Dura, in the province of Babylon. [2] Then Nebuchadnezzar the king sent to gather together the princes, the governors, and the captains, the judges, the treasurers, the counsellors, the sheriffs, and all the rulers of the provinces, to come to the dedication of the image which Nebuchadnezzar

the king had set up. ³ Then the princes, the governors, and captains, the judges, the treasurers, the counsellors, the sheriffs, and all the rulers of the provinces, were gathered together unto the dedication of the image that Nebuchadnezzar the king had set up; and they stood before the image that Nebuchadnezzar had set up. ⁴ Then an herald cried aloud, To you it is commanded, O people, nations, and languages, ⁵ That at what time ye hear the sound of the cornet, flute, harp, sackbut, psaltery, dulcimer, and all kinds of musick, ye fall down and worship the golden image that Nebuchadnezzar the king hath set up: ⁶ And whoso falleth not down and worshippeth shall the same hour be cast into the midst of a burning fiery furnace. ⁷ Therefore at that time, when all the people heard the sound of the cornet, flute, harp, sackbut, psaltery, and all kinds of musick, all the people, the nations, and the languages, fell down and worshipped the golden image that Nebuchadnezzar the king had set up. ⁸ Wherefore at that time certain Chaldeans came near, and accused the Jews. ⁹ They spake and said to the king Nebuchadnezzar, O king, live for ever. ¹⁰ Thou, O king, hast made a decree, that every man that shall hear the sound of the cornet, flute, harp, sackbut, psaltery, and dulcimer, and all kinds of musick, shall fall down and worship the golden image: ¹¹ And whoso falleth not down and worshippeth, that he should be cast into the midst of a burning fiery furnace. ¹² There are certain Jews whom thou hast set over the affairs of the province of Babylon, Shadrach, Meshach, and Abednego; these men, O king, have not regarded thee: they serve not thy gods, nor worship the golden image which thou hast set up. ¹³ Then Nebuchadnezzar in his rage and fury commanded to bring Shadrach, Meshach, and Abednego. Then they brought these men before the king. ¹⁴ Nebuchadnezzar spake and said unto them, Is it true, O Shadrach, Meshach, and Abednego, do not ye serve my gods, nor worship the golden image which I have set up? ¹⁵ Now if ye be ready that at what time ye hear the sound of the cornet, flute, harp, sackbut, psaltery, and dulcimer, and all kinds of musick, ye fall down and worship the image which I have made; well: but if ye worship not, ye shall be cast the same hour into the midst of a burning fiery furnace; and who is that God that shall deliver you out of my hands? ¹⁶ Shadrach, Meshach, and Abednego, answered and said to the king, O Nebuchadnezzar, we are not careful to answer thee in this matter. ¹⁷ If it be so, our God whom we serve is able to deliver us from the burning fiery furnace, and he will deliver us out of thine hand, O king. ¹⁸ But if not, be it known unto thee, O king, that we will not serve thy gods, nor worship the golden image which thou hast set up. ¹⁹ Then was Nebuchadnezzar full of fury, and the form of his visage was changed against Shadrach, Meshach, and Abednego: therefore he spake, and commanded that they should heat the furnace one seven times more than it was wont to be heated. ²⁰ And he commanded the most mighty men that were in his army to bind Shadrach, Meshach, and Abednego, and to cast them into the burning fiery furnace. ²¹ Then these men were bound in their coats, their hosen, and their hats, and their other garments, and were cast into the midst of the burning fiery furnace. ²² Therefore because the king's commandment was urgent, and the furnace exceeding hot, the flames of the fire slew those men that took up Shadrach, Meshach, and Abednego. ²³ And these three men, Shadrach, Meshach, and Abednego, fell down bound into the midst of the burning fiery furnace. ²⁴ Then Nebuchadnezzar the king was astonished, and rose up in haste, and spake, and said unto his counsellors, Did not we cast three men bound into the midst of the fire? They answered and said unto the king, True, O king. ²⁵ He answered and said, Lo, I see four men loose, walking in the midst of the fire, and they have no hurt; and the form of the fourth is like the Son of God. ²⁶ Then Nebuchadnezzar came near to the mouth of the burning fiery furnace, and spake, and said, Shadrach, Meshach, and Abednego, ye servants of the most high God, come forth, and come hither. Then Shadrach, Meshach, and Abednego, came forth of the midst of the fire. ²⁷ And the princes, governors, and captains, and the king's counsellors, being gathered together, saw these men, upon whose bodies the fire had no power, nor was an hair of their head singed, neither were their coats changed, nor the smell of fire had passed on them. ²⁸ Then Nebuchadnezzar spake, and said, Blessed be the God of Shadrach, Meshach, and Abednego, who hath sent his angel, and delivered his servants that trusted in him, and have changed the king's word, and yielded their bodies, that they might not serve nor worship any god, except their own God. ²⁹ Therefore I make a decree, That every people, nation, and language, which speak any thing amiss against the God of Shadrach, Meshach, and Abednego, shall be cut in pieces, and their houses shall be made a dunghill: because there is no other God that can deliver after this sort. ³⁰ Then the king promoted Shadrach, Meshach, and Abednego, in the province of Babylon. (Page 2)

Chapter 1

Hebrews 11:25
Choosing rather to suffer affliction with the people of God, than to enjoy the pleasures of sin for a season. (Page 7)

Romans 7:15
For that which I do I allow not: for what I would, that do I not; but what I hate, that do I. (Page 7)

Chapter 2

James 1:14
But every man is tempted, when he is drawn away of his own lust, and enticed. (Page 10)

Proverbs 20:11
Even a child is known by his doings, whether his work be pure, and whether it be right. (Page 11)

James 5:16
Confess your faults one to another, and pray one for another, that ye may be healed. The effectual fervent prayer of a righteous man availeth much. (Page 12)

Chapter 3

Jeremiah 1:5
Before I formed thee in the belly I knew thee; and before thou camest forth out of the womb I sanctified thee, and I ordained thee a prophet unto the nations. (Pages 15 and 19)

Proverbs 18:21
Death and life are in the power of the tongue: and they that love it shall eat the fruit thereof. (Page 17)

Isaiah 55:8-9
⁸"For my thoughts are not your thoughts, neither are your ways my ways," saith the LORD. ⁹"For as the heavens are higher than the earth, so are my ways higher than your ways, and my thoughts than your thoughts." (Page 17)

Scriptures Used or Referenced

Proverbs 3:5
Trust in the Lord with all thine heart; and lean not unto thine own understanding. (Page 18)

John 9:31
Now we know that God heareth not sinners: but if any man be a worshipper of God, and doeth his will, him he heareth. (Page 18)

Psalm 51:17
The sacrifices of God are a broken spirit: a broken and a contrite heart, O God, thou wilt not despise. (Pages 18 and 19)

Chapter 4

Ephesians 6:11-13
[11] Put on the whole armour of God, that ye may be able to stand against the wiles of the devil. [12] For we wrestle not against flesh and blood, but against principalities, against powers, against the rulers of the darkness of this world, against spiritual wickedness in high places. [13] Wherefore take unto you the whole armour of God, that ye may be able to withstand in the evil day, and having done all, to stand. (Page 24)

Chapter 5

Ezekiel 36:26-27
[26] A new heart also will I give you, and a new spirit will I put within you: and I will take away the stony heart out of your flesh, and I will give you an heart of flesh. [27] And I will put my spirit within you, and cause you to walk in my statues, and ye shall keep my judgments, and do them. (Page 25)

Romans 6:14
For sin shall not have dominion over you: for ye are not under the law, but under grace. (Page 25)

1 Corinthians 10:13
There hath no temptation taken you but such as is common to man: but God is faithful, who will not suffer you to be tempted above that ye are able; but will with the temptation also make a way to escape. (Page 25)

Galatians 5:17
For the flesh lusteth against the Spirit, and the Spirit against the flesh: and

these are contrary the one to the other: so that ye cannot do the things that ye would. (Page 25)

Acts 7:58-60
⁵⁸ And cast him out of the city, and stoned him: and the witnesses laid down their clothes at a young man's feet, whose name was Saul. ⁵⁹ And they stoned Stephen, calling upon God, and saying, Lord Jesus, receive my spirit. ⁶⁰ And he kneeled down, and cried with a loud voice, Lord, lay not this sin to their charge. And when he had said this, he fell asleep. (Page 25)

Acts 6:1-3
¹And in those days, when the number of the disciples was multiplied, there arose a murmuring of the Grecians against the Hebrews, because their widows were neglected in the daily ministration. ² Then the twelve called the multitude of the disciples unto them, and said, It is not reason that we should leave the word of God, and serve tables. ³ Wherefore, brethren, look ye out among you seven men of honest report, full of the Holy Ghost and wisdom, whom we may appoint over this business. (Page 26)

Acts 6:8
And Stephen, full of faith and power, did great wonders and miracles among the people. (Page 26)

Acts 8:3
As for Saul, he made havock of the church, entering into every house, and haling men and women committed them to prison. (Page 26)

Acts 9:1-6
¹And Saul, yet breathing out threatenings and slaughter against the disciples of the Lord, went unto the high priest, ² And desired of him letters to Damascus to the synagogues, that if he found any of this way, whether they were men or women, he might bring them bound unto Jerusalem. ³ And as he journeyed, he came near Damascus: and suddenly there shined round about him a light from heaven: ⁴ And he fell to the earth, and heard a voice saying unto him, Saul, Saul, why persecutest thou me? ⁵ And he said, Who art thou, Lord? And the Lord said, I am Jesus whom thou persecutest: it is hard for thee to kick against the pricks. ⁶ And he trembling and astonished said, Lord, what wilt thou have me to do? And the Lord said unto him, Arise, and go into the city, and it shall be told

thee what thou must do. (Page 26)

2 Corinthians 5:17
Therefore if any man be in Christ, he is a new creature: old things are passed away; behold, all things are become new. (Page 26)

Proverbs 27:17
Iron sharpeneth iron; so a man sharpeneth the countenance of his friend. (Page 28)

Chapter 6

Proverbs 16:9
A man's heart deviseth his way, but the Lord directeth his steps. (Pages 30 and 34)

Proverbs 19:21
There are many devices in a man's heart; nevertheless the counsel of the Lord, that shall stand. (Pages 30 and 34)

Luke 7:37-39
[37] And, behold, a woman in the city, which was a sinner, when she knew that Jesus sat at meat in the Pharisee's house, brought an alabaster box of ointment, [38] And stood at his feet behind him weeping, and began to wash his feet with tears, and did wipe them with the hairs of her head, and kissed his feet, and anointed them with the ointment. [39] Now when the Pharisee which had bidden him saw it, he spake within himself, saying, This man, if he were a prophet, would have known who and what manner of woman this is that toucheth him: for she is a sinner. (Page 31)

Luke 7:47
Wherefore I say unto thee, Her sins, which are many, are forgiven; for she loved much: but to whom little is forgiven, the same loveth little. (Page 31)

Genesis 2:24
Therefore shall a man leave his father and his mother, and shall cleave unto his wife: and they shall be one flesh. (Page 32)

Chapter 7

Malachi 2:16
For the LORD, the God of Israel, saith that he hateth putting away: for one

covereth violence with his garment, saith the LORD of hosts: therefore take heed to your spirit, that ye deal not treacherously. (Page 35)

Matthew 5:32
But I say unto you, That whosoever shall put away his wife, saving for the cause of fornication, causeth her to commit adultery: and whosoever shall marry her that is divorced committeth adultery. (Page 35)

Matthew 19:9
And I say unto you, Whosoever shall put away his wife, except it be for fornication, and shall marry another, committeth adultery: and whoso marrieth her which is put away doth commit adultery. (Page 35)

1 Corinthians 7:15
But if the unbelieving depart, let him depart. A brother or a sister is not under bondage in such cases: but God hath called us to peace. (Page 35)

Matthew 5:14
Ye are the light of the world. A city that is set on an hill cannot be hid. (Page 35)

Matthew 19:8
He saith unto them, Moses because of the hardness of your hearts suffered you to put away your wives: but from the beginning it was not so. (Pages 35-36)

Genesis 2:24
Therefore shall a man leave his father and his mother, and shall cleave unto his wife: and they shall be one flesh.(Page 36)

Matthew 19:5-6
[5] And said, For this cause shall a man leave father and mother, and shall cleave to his wife: and they twain shall be one flesh? [6] Wherefore they are no more twain, but one flesh. What therefore God hath joined together, let not man put asunder. (Page 36)

Luke 6:36-38
[36] Be ye therefore merciful, as your Father also is merciful. [37] Judge not, and ye shall not be judged: condemn not, and ye shall not be condemned: forgive, and ye shall be forgiven: [38] Give, and it shall be given unto you; good measure, pressed down, and shaken together, and running over, shall men give into your bosom. For with the same measure that ye mete

withal it shall be measured to you again. (Page 39)

<u>Chapter 8</u>

1 Corinthians 11:3

But I would have you know, that the head of every man is Christ; and the head of the woman is the man; and the head of Christ is God. (Page 41)

Ephesians 5:25-28

[25] Husbands, love your wives, even as Christ also loved the church, and gave himself for it; [26] That he might sanctify and cleanse it with the washing of water by the word, [27] That he might present it to himself a glorious church, not having spot, or wrinkle, or any such thing; but that it should be holy and without blemish. [28] So ought men to love their wives as their own bodies. He that loveth his wife loveth himself. (Page 41)

John 10:10

The thief cometh not, but for to steal, and to kill, and to destroy: I am come that they might have life, and that they might have it more abundantly. (Page 41)

1 Corinthians 6:15-20

[15] Know ye not that your bodies are the members of Christ? shall I then take the members of Christ, and make them the members of an harlot? God forbid. [16] What? know ye not that he which is joined to an harlot is one body? for two, saith he, shall be one flesh. [17] But he that is joined unto the Lord is one spirit. [18] Flee fornication. Every sin that a man doeth is without the body; but he that committeth fornication sinneth against his own body. [19] What? know ye not that your body is the temple of the Holy Ghost which is in you, which ye have of God, and ye are not your own? [20] For ye are bought with a price: therefore glorify God in your body, and in your spirit, which are God's. (Pages 42 and 45)

Luke 12:47-48

[47] And that servant, which knew his lord's will, and prepared not himself, neither did according to his will, shall be beaten with many stripes. [48] But he that knew not, and did commit things worthy of stripes, shall be beaten with few stripes. For unto whomsoever much is given, of him shall be much required: and to whom men have committed much, of him they will ask the more. (Page 43)

James 3:1
My brethren, be not many masters, knowing that we shall receive the greater condemnation. (Page 43)

1 Corinthians 5
^{1} It is reported commonly that there is fornication among you, and such fornication as is not so much as named among the Gentiles, that one should have his father's wife. ^{2} And ye are puffed up, and have not rather mourned, that he that hath done this deed might be taken away from among you. ^{3} For I verily, as absent in body, but present in spirit, have judged already, as though I were present, concerning him that hath so done this deed, ^{4} In the name of our Lord Jesus Christ, when ye are gathered together, and my spirit, with the power of our Lord Jesus Christ, ^{5} To deliver such an one unto Satan for the destruction of the flesh, that the spirit may be saved in the day of the Lord Jesus. ^{6} Your glorying is not good. Know ye not that a little leaven leaveneth the whole lump? ^{7} Purge out therefore the old leaven, that ye may be a new lump, as ye are unleavened. For even Christ our passover is sacrificed for us: ^{8} Therefore let us keep the feast, not with old leaven, neither with the leaven of malice and wickedness; but with the unleavened bread of sincerity and truth. ^{9} I wrote unto you in an epistle not to company with fornicators: ^{10} Yet not altogether with the fornicators of this world, or with the covetous, or extortioners, or with idolaters; for then must ye needs go out of the world. ^{11} But now I have written unto you not to keep company, if any man that is called a brother be a fornicator, or covetous, or an idolator, or a railer, or a drunkard, or an extortioner; with such an one no not to eat. ^{12} For what have I to do to judge them also that are without? do not ye judge them that are within? ^{13} But them that are without God judgeth. Therefore put away from among yourselves that wicked person. (Pages 43 and 45)

1 Corinthians 6:18
Flee fornication. Every sin that a man doeth is without the body; but he that committeth fornication sinneth against his own body. (Pages 43)

Romans 6:1-2
^{1} What shall we say then? Shall we continue in sin, that grace may abound?

² God forbid. How shall we, that are dead to sin, live any longer therein? (Page 45)

Chapter 9

Genesis 18:10-12
¹⁰ And he said, I will certainly return unto thee according to the time of life; and, lo, Sarah thy wife shall have a son. And Sarah heard it in the tent door, which was behind him. ¹¹ Now Abraham and Sarah were old and well stricken in age; and it ceased to be with Sarah after the manner of women. ¹² Therefore Sarah laughed within herself, saying, After I am waxed old shall I have pleasure, my lord being old also? (Page 47)

Proverbs 16:9
A man's heart deviseth his way, but the Lord directeth his steps. (Page 48)

Proverbs 19:21
There are many devices in a man's heart; nevertheless the counsel of the Lord, that shall stand. (Page 48)

Chapter 10

Genesis 2:18
And the LORD God said, It is not good that the man should be alone; I will make him an help meet for him. (Page 54)

1 Timothy 5:8
But if any provide not for his own, and specially for those of his own house, he hath denied the faith, and is worse than an infidel. (Page 55)

Chapter 11

Philippians 3:13-14
¹³ Brethren, I count not myself to have apprehended: but this one thing I do, forgetting those things which are behind, and reaching forth unto those things which are before, ¹⁴ I press toward the mark for the prize of the high calling of God in Christ Jesus. (Page 58)

Luke 12:48
But he that knew not, and did commit things worthy of stripes, shall be beaten with few stripes. For unto whomsoever much is given, of him shall be much required: and to whom men have committed much, of him they

will ask the more. (Page 61)

1 Corinthians 6:1-8
¹ Dare any of you, having a matter against another, go to law before the unjust, and not before the saints? ² Do ye not know that the saints shall judge the world? and if the world shall be judged by you, are ye unworthy to judge the smallest matters? ³ Know ye not that we shall judge angels? how much more things that pertain to this life? ⁴ If then ye have judgments of things pertaining to this life, set them to judge who are least esteemed in the church. ⁵ I speak to your shame. Is it so, that there is not a wise man among you? no, not one that shall be able to judge between his brethren? ⁶ But brother goeth to law with brother, and that before the unbelievers. ⁷ Now therefore there is utterly a fault among you, because ye go to law one with another. Why do ye not rather take wrong? why do ye not rather suffer yourselves to be defrauded? ⁸ Nay, ye do wrong, and defraud, and that your brethren. (Page 61)

Chapter 12

Isaiah 38:1
In those days was Hezekiah sick unto death. And Isaiah the prophet the son of Amoz came unto him, and said unto him, Thus saith the Lord, Set thine house in order: for thou shalt die, and not live. (Page 63)

Chapter 13

John 9:1-3
¹And as Jesus passed by, he saw a man which was blind from his birth. ²And his disciples asked him, saying, "Master, who did sin, this man, or his parents, that he was born blind?" ³Jesus answered, "Neither hath this man sinned, nor his parents: but that the works of God should be made manifest in him." (Page 69)

Proverbs 3:5-6
⁵Trust in the Lord with all thine heart; and lean not unto thine own understanding. ⁶In all thy ways acknowledge him, and he shall direct thy paths. (Page 69)

Romans 8:28
And we know that all things work together for good to them that love

God, to them who are the called according to his purpose. (Pages 69 and 76)

1 Corinthians 15:58
Therefore, my beloved brethren, be ye stedfast, unmoveable, always abounding in the work of the Lord, forasmuch as ye know that your labour is not in vain in the Lord. (Page 70)

1 Corinthians 5:1-8
[1] It is reported commonly that there is fornication among you, and such fornication as is not so much as named among the Gentiles, that one should have his father's wife. [2] And ye are puffed up, and have not rather mourned, that he that hath done this deed might be taken away from among you. [3] For I verily, as absent in body, but present in spirit, have judged already, as though I were present, concerning him that hath so done this deed, [4] In the name of our Lord Jesus Christ, when ye are gathered together, and my spirit, with the power of our Lord Jesus Christ, [5] To deliver such an one unto Satan for the destruction of the flesh, that the spirit may be saved in the day of the Lord Jesus. [6] Your glorying is not good. Know ye not that a little leaven leaveneth the whole lump? [7] Purge out therefore the old leaven, that ye may be a new lump, as ye are unleavened. For even Christ our passover is sacrificed for us: [8] Therefore let us keep the feast, not with old leaven, neither with the leaven of malice and wickedness; but with the unleavened bread of sincerity and truth. (Page 71)

2 Corinthians 2:3-11
[3] And I wrote this same unto you, lest, when I came, I should have sorrow from them of whom I ought to rejoice; having confidence in you all, that my joy is the joy of you all. [4] For out of much affliction and anguish of heart I wrote unto you with many tears; not that ye should be grieved, but that ye might know the love which I have more abundantly unto you. [5] But if any have caused grief, he hath not grieved me, but in part: that I may not overcharge you all. [6] Sufficient to such a man is this punishment, which was inflicted of many. [7] So that contrariwise ye ought rather to forgive him, and comfort him, lest perhaps such a one should be swallowed up with overmuch sorrow. [8] Wherefore I beseech you that ye would confirm your love toward him. [9] For to this end also did I write,

that I might know the proof of you, whether ye be obedient in all things. ¹⁰ To whom ye forgive any thing, I forgive also: for if I forgave any thing, to whom I forgave it, for your sakes forgave I it in the person of Christ; ¹¹ Lest Satan should get an advantage of us: for we are not ignorant of his devices. (Page 71)

Matthew 18:15-17
¹⁵ Moreover if thy brother shall trespass against thee, go and tell him his fault between thee and him alone: if he shall hear thee, thou hast gained thy brother. ¹⁶ But if he will not hear thee, then take with thee one or two more, that in the mouth of two or three witnesses every word may be established. ¹⁷ And if he shall neglect to hear them, tell it unto the church: but if he neglect to hear the church, let him be unto thee as an heathen man and a publican. (Page 71)

2 Corinthians 5:17
Therefore if any man be in Christ, he is a new creature: old things are passed away; behold, all things are become new. (Page 76)

Chapter 14

Luke 23:20-21
²⁰ Pilate therefore, willing to release Jesus, spake again to them. ²¹ But they cried, saying, Crucify him, crucify him. (Page 79)

Proverbs 29:18
Where there is no vision, the people perish: but he that keepeth the law, happy is he. (Page 79)

Nehemiah 4
⁴ But it came to pass, that when Sanballat heard that we builded the wall, he was wroth, and took great indignation, and mocked the Jews. ² And he spake before his brethren and the army of Samaria, and said, What do these feeble Jews? will they fortify themselves? will they sacrifice? will they make an end in a day? will they revive the stones out of the heaps of the rubbish which are burned? ³ Now Tobiah the Ammonite was by him, and he said, Even that which they build, if a fox go up, he shall even break down their stone wall.⁴ Hear, O our God; for we are despised: and turn their reproach upon their own head, and give them for a prey in the land of captivity: ⁵ And cover not their iniquity, and let not their sin be blotted

out from before thee: for they have provoked thee to anger before the builders. ⁶ So built we the wall; and all the wall was joined together unto the half thereof: for the people had a mind to work. ⁷ But it came to pass, that when Sanballat, and Tobiah, and the Arabians, and the Ammonites, and the Ashdodites, heard that the walls of Jerusalem were made up, and that the breaches began to be stopped, then they were very wroth, ⁸ And conspired all of them together to come and to fight against Jerusalem, and to hinder it. ⁹ Nevertheless we made our prayer unto our God, and set a watch against them day and night, because of them. ¹⁰ And Judah said, The strength of the bearers of burdens is decayed, and there is much rubbish; so that we are not able to build the wall. ¹¹ And our adversaries said, They shall not know, neither see, till we come in the midst among them, and slay them, and cause the work to cease. ¹² And it came to pass, that when the Jews which dwelt by them came, they said unto us ten times, From all places whence ye shall return unto us they will be upon you. ¹³ Therefore set I in the lower places behind the wall, and on the higher places, I even set the people after their families with their swords, their spears, and their bows. ¹⁴ And I looked, and rose up, and said unto the nobles, and to the rulers, and to the rest of the people, Be not ye afraid of them: remember the LORD, which is great and terrible, and fight for your brethren, your sons, and your daughters, your wives, and your houses. ¹⁵ And it came to pass, when our enemies heard that it was known unto us, and God had brought their counsel to nought, that we returned all of us to the wall, every one unto his work. ¹⁶ And it came to pass from that time forth, that the half of my servants wrought in the work, and the other half of them held both the spears, the shields, and the bows, and the habergeons; and the rulers were behind all the house of Judah. ¹⁷ They which builded on the wall, and they that bare burdens, with those that laded, every one with one of his hands wrought in the work, and with the other hand held a weapon. ¹⁸ For the builders, every one had his sword girded by his side, and so builded. And he that sounded the trumpet was by me. ¹⁹ And I said unto the nobles, and to the rulers, and to the rest of the people, The work is great and large, and we are separated upon the wall, one far from another. ²⁰ In what place therefore ye hear the sound of the trumpet, resort ye thither unto us: our God shall fight for us. ²¹ So we laboured in the work: and half of them held the spears from the rising of the morning till the stars appeared. [22] Likewise at the same time said I unto the people, Let every one with his servant lodge within Jerusalem, that in the night they may be a guard to us, and labour on the day. [23] So neither I, nor my brethren, nor my servants, nor the men of the guard which followed me, none of us put off our clothes, saving that every one put them off for washing. (Pages 79 and 80)

Matthew 5:16
Let your light so shine before men, that they may see your good works, and glorify your Father which is in heaven. (Page 81)

Chapter 15

Philippians 4:7
And the peace of God, which passeth all understanding, shall keep your hearts and minds through Christ Jesus.(Page 83)

James 1:2
My brethren, count it all joy when ye fall into divers temptations. (Page 83)

John 8:36
If the Son therefore shall make you free, ye shall be free indeed. (Page 85)

Conclusion

Psalm 139
[1] O lord, thou hast searched me, and known me. [2] Thou knowest my downsitting and mine uprising, thou understandest my thought afar off. [3] Thou compassest my path and my lying down, and art acquainted with all my ways. [4] For there is not a word in my tongue, but, lo, O Lord, thou knowest it altogether. [5] Thou hast beset me behind and before, and laid thine hand upon me. [6] Such knowledge is too wonderful for me; it is high, I cannot attain unto it. [7] Whither shall I go from thy spirit? or whither shall I flee from thy presence? [8] If I ascend up into heaven, thou art there: if I make my bed in hell, behold, thou art there. [9] If I take the wings of the morning, and dwell in the uttermost parts of the sea; [10] Even there shall thy hand lead me, and thy right hand shall hold me. [11] If I say, Surely the darkness shall cover me; even the night shall be light about me. [12] Yea, the darkness hideth not from thee; but the night shineth as the day: the darkness and the light are both alike to thee. [13] For thou hast possessed

my reins: thou hast covered me in my mother's womb. [14] I will praise thee; for I am fearfully and wonderfully made: marvellous are thy works; and that my soul knoweth right well. [15] My substance was not hid from thee, when I was made in secret, and curiously wrought in the lowest parts of the earth. [16] Thine eyes did see my substance, yet being unperfect; and in thy book all my members were written, which in continuance were fashioned, when as yet there was none of them. [17] How precious also are thy thoughts unto me, O God! how great is the sum of them! [18] If I should count them, they are more in number than the sand: when I awake, I am still with thee. [19] Surely thou wilt slay the wicked, O God: depart from me therefore, ye bloody men. [20] For they speak against thee wickedly, and thine enemies take thy name in vain. [21] Do not I hate them, O Lord, that hate thee? and am not I grieved with those that rise up against thee? [22] I hate them with perfect hatred: I count them mine enemies. [23] Search me, O God, and know my heart: try me, and know my thoughts: [24] And see if there be any wicked way in me, and lead me in the way everlasting. (Pages 87 and 92)

Proverbs 12:19
The lip of truth shall be established for ever: but a lying tongue is but for a moment. (Page 88)

Psalm 23:5
Thou prepares a table before me in the presence of mine enemies: though anointest my head with oil; my cup runneth over. (Page 88)

Matthew 5:9
Blessed are the peacemakers: for they shall be called the children of God. (Page 89)

Hebrews 10:38
Now the just shall live by faith: but if any man draw back, my soul shall have no pleasure in him. (Page 90)

Romans 12:17 Recompense to no man evil for evil. Provide things honest in the sight of all men. (Page 90)

1 Peter 3:9
Not rendering evil for evil, or railing for railing: but contrariwise blessing;

knowing that ye are thereunto called, that ye should inherit a blessing. (Page 90)

Proverbs 10:12
Hatred stirreth up strifes: but love covereth all sins. (Page 90)

1 Peter 4:8
And above all things have fervent charity among yourselves: for charity shall cover the multitude of sins. (Page 90)

Daniel 3
[1] Nebuchadnezzar the king made an image of gold, whose height was threescore cubits, and the breadth thereof six cubits: he set it up in the plain of Dura, in the province of Babylon. [2] Then Nebuchadnezzar the king sent to gather together the princes, the governors, and the captains, the judges, the treasurers, the counsellors, the sheriffs, and all the rulers of the provinces, to come to the dedication of the image which Nebuchadnezzar the king had set up. [3] Then the princes, the governors, and captains, the judges, the treasurers, the counsellors, the sheriffs, and all the rulers of the provinces, were gathered together unto the dedication of the image that Nebuchadnezzar the king had set up; and they stood before the image that Nebuchadnezzar had set up. [4] Then an herald cried aloud, To you it is commanded, O people, nations, and languages, [5] That at what time ye hear the sound of the cornet, flute, harp, sackbut, psaltery, dulcimer, and all kinds of musick, ye fall down and worship the golden image that Nebuchadnezzar the king hath set up: [6] And whoso falleth not down and worshippeth shall the same hour be cast into the midst of a burning fiery furnace. [7] Therefore at that time, when all the people heard the sound of the cornet, flute, harp, sackbut, psaltery, and all kinds of musick, all the people, the nations, and the languages, fell down and worshipped the golden image that Nebuchadnezzar the king had set up. [8] Wherefore at that time certain Chaldeans came near, and accused the Jews. [9] They spake and said to the king Nebuchadnezzar, O king, live for ever. [10] Thou, O king, hast made a decree, that every man that shall hear the sound of the cornet, flute, harp, sackbut, psaltery, and dulcimer, and all kinds of musick, shall fall down and worship the golden image: [11] And whoso falleth not down and worshippeth, that he should be cast into the midst of a burning fiery furnace. [12] There are certain Jews whom thou hast set over the affairs of the province of Babylon, Shadrach, Meshach, and Abednego; these

men, O king, have not regarded thee: they serve not thy gods, nor worship the golden image which thou hast set up. ¹³ Then Nebuchadnezzar in his rage and fury commanded to bring Shadrach, Meshach, and Abednego. Then they brought these men before the king. ¹⁴ Nebuchadnezzar spake and said unto them, Is it true, O Shadrach, Meshach, and Abednego, do not ye serve my gods, nor worship the golden image which I have set up? ¹⁵ Now if ye be ready that at what time ye hear the sound of the cornet, flute, harp, sackbut, psaltery, and dulcimer, and all kinds of musick, ye fall down and worship the image which I have made; well: but if ye worship not, ye shall be cast the same hour into the midst of a burning fiery furnace; and who is that God that shall deliver you out of my hands? ¹⁶ Shadrach, Meshach, and Abednego, answered and said to the king, O Nebuchadnezzar, we are not careful to answer thee in this matter. ¹⁷ If it be so, our God whom we serve is able to deliver us from the burning fiery furnace, and he will deliver us out of thine hand, O king. ¹⁸ But if not, be it known unto thee, O king, that we will not serve thy gods, nor worship the golden image which thou hast set up. ¹⁹ Then was Nebuchadnezzar full of fury, and the form of his visage was changed against Shadrach, Meshach, and Abednego: therefore he spake, and commanded that they should heat the furnace one seven times more than it was wont to be heated. ²⁰ And he commanded the most mighty men that were in his army to bind Shadrach, Meshach, and Abednego, and to cast them into the burning fiery furnace. ²¹ Then these men were bound in their coats, their hosen, and their hats, and their other garments, and were cast into the midst of the burning fiery furnace. ²² Therefore because the king's commandment was urgent, and the furnace exceeding hot, the flames of the fire slew those men that took up Shadrach, Meshach, and Abednego. ²³ And these three men, Shadrach, Meshach, and Abednego, fell down bound into the midst of the burning fiery furnace. ²⁴ Then Nebuchadnezzar the king was astonished, and rose up in haste, and spake, and said unto his counsellors, Did not we cast three men bound into the midst of the fire? They answered and said unto the king, True, O king. ²⁵ He answered and said, Lo, I see four men loose, walking in the midst of the fire, and they have no hurt; and the form of the fourth is like the Son of God. ²⁶ Then Nebuchadnezzar came near to the mouth of the burning fiery furnace, and spake, and said, Shadrach, Meshach, and Abednego, ye servants of the most high God, come forth, and come hither. Then Shadrach, Meshach, and Abednego, came forth of the midst of the fire. ²⁷ And the princes, governors, and captains, and the king's counsellors, being gathered together, saw these men, upon whose bodies the fire had no power, nor was an hair of their head singed, neither were their coats changed, nor the smell of fire had passed on them. ²⁸ Then Nebuchadnezzar spake, and said, Blessed be the God of Shadrach, Meshach, and Abednego, who hath sent his angel, and delivered his servants that trusted in him, and have changed the king's word, and yielded their bodies, that they might not serve nor worship any god, except their own God. ²⁹ Therefore I make a decree, That every people, nation, and language, which speak any thing amiss against the God of Shadrach, Meshach, and Abednego, shall be cut in pieces, and their houses shall be made a dunghill: because there is no other God that can deliver after this sort. ³⁰ Then the king promoted Shadrach, Meshach, and Abednego, in the province of Babylon. (Page 92)

Appendix A

Romans 10:9-10
⁹ That if thou shalt confess with thy mouth the Lord Jesus, and shalt believe in thine heart that God hath raised him from the dead, thou shalt be saved. ¹⁰ For with the heart man believeth unto righteousness; and with the mouth confession is made unto salvation. (Page 93)

Luke 15:10
Likewise, I say unto you, there is joy in the presence of the angels of God over one sinner that repenteth. (Page 93)

Appendix C: Letter of "Support"

Below is a more legible version of the letter on page 74 that was sent to my wife. It was re-typed verbatim. Thus, no grammar, spelling, or punctuation corrections have been made.

Sister Brenda Gardner Howard
Memphis, TN. 38141-0248

April 18, 2012

Dear Sister Brenda Haith-Howard,

There are not enough words to describe how precious Pastors are, but unfortunately your husband does not fit into that category. It seems you were in on it all the time. You were in "co-hoots" with your crooked spouse to rob and destroy our fine church. As we look upon you with pity, we wonder just what were you thinking about this so called man of God you have dropped off on us. We want you to TAKE him back with you and keep him down there with you.

Please know this one thing however; that we know you are an abused women and is still greatly in need of prayer, but your need does not give you the right to take our kindness for a weakness, to benefit your pimp wannabe preacher husband.

We will rid ourselves of him and hope not to see you anymore. As we worship with your husband and look at this crook perform every Sunday, know this one thang..... We hate him for what he stands for and for what he has and is doing to our church. The extensive background investigation has uncovered and exposed all of his illusive, deceptive, carnal, and apostate carrying on. How dare he come to Ebenezer with all of this witchery baggage to destroy, scatter and separate? Did you and "Tanyhill" think you had struck pay dirt once your eyes feasted on our finances? Yes, we do know about Tanyhill and all of his crimes. Yes, we do know about the destruction of his last 3 churches and the robbery of God that went along with his schemes.

The theme for your anniversary "Fulfillment of the Great Commission" could not have come at a better time, or maybe at a very inopportune time. Look at God and how the fulfillment of the GREAT COMMISSION is working. You have confessed to know the bible and God's word, so direct your attention to Mark chapter 13 and St. John chapter 14 and 17. These messages are from God. Watch for the things that are coming! Stand on HIS word! And lastly, this battle is the LORD'S!!

May God Himself, reward him for his deeds.

Prayerfully,

Your support at Ebenezer

Your support at Ebenezer

Endnotes

1. Our Mt. Vernon Neighborhood - CSCC Library's Art Collection - Research Guides at Columbus State Community College." About Us - Welcome to the Library - Research Guides at Columbus State Community College. Accessed May 21, 2015. http://library.cscc.edu/c.php?g=126555&p=827830.
2. "Phenmetrazine," MedLibrary.org, accessed May 21, 2015, http://medlibrary.org/medwiki/Phenmetrazine.
3. Stirring Response. (n.d.). Retrieved May 23, 2015, from http://www.snopes.com/business/origins/mcdspoon.asp
4. "National Baptist Convention - Envisioning the Future Exceptionally - Congress of Christian Education." National Baptist Convention - Envisioning the Future Exceptionally - Congress of Christian Education. Accessed May 22, 2015. http://www.nationalbaptist.com/meetings--events/congress-of-christian-education/.
5. "What Is Palm Sunday." What Is Palm Sunday. Accessed May 22, 2015. http://www.sharefaith.com/guide/Christian-Holidays/what-is-palm-sunday.html.
6. Warren Buffett. BrainyQuote.com, Xplore Inc, 2015. Accessed May 22, 2015. http://www.brainyquote.com/quotes/quotes/w/warrenbuff108887.html.
7. "The Roller Coaster Capital of the World | Cedar Point." The Roller Coaster Capital of the World | Cedar Point. Accessed May 22, 2015. https://www.cedarpoint.com/
8. The Jackson Southernaires, "Run on, See What the Ends Gonna Be," in *Lead Me,* Malaco Inc, 1983, https://itunes.apple.com/us/album/lead-me/id102492655

About the Publisher

Yo Productions, LLC was founded by *Essence* bestselling author, Yolonda Tonette Sanders in 2008. Initially, Yolonda started the company to produce a stage adaptation of her first book, *Soul Matters*. Over the years, Yo Productions has grown into a multi-faceted organization.

As a **literary services** provider, Yo Productions specializes in proofreading, editing, ghostwriting, and consulting, among other things, in order to address individual client needs. Once a year, the company hosts a weekend women's retreat (Weekend Writeaway) to encourage relaxation and creativity among established and aspiring authors. In addition, creative writing workshops are offered at various times throughout the year for both men and women.

As a **theatrical entertainment** provider, Yo Productions aims to produce thought-provoking, dramatic performances that reach people from all walks of life. The company's motto, "Performance with Purpose," stems from the founder's desire to create and produce works that have meaning far beyond simply entertaining audiences.

As a **publisher**, Yo Productions operates under a traditional model as a full-fledged publishing house that assumes the financial costs of editing, printing, and distributing works created by its authors. The company focuses on both digital and print releases. Paperback copies of books released under this imprint are available through a print-on-demand service and are accessible to over 38,000 retail outlets, including online sellers such as Amazon and Barnes and Noble. Yo Productions prides itself on being attentive to individual author needs and on treating every book like a bestseller. For more information or to submit your work for consideration, please visit www.yoproductions.net.

www.ingramcontent.com/pod-product-compliance
Lightning Source LLC
Chambersburg PA
CBHW031423290426
44110CB00011B/501